LAKE COUNTRY
ECHOES

12 msc   S86701

"The roots of the present lie deep in the past, and nothing in the past is dead to the man who would learn how the present comes to be what it is ."

Stubbs.

LAKE COUNTRY ECHOES

NORTH COUNTRY PEOPLE AND PLACES

———

H. A. L. RICE

———

KENDAL
WESTMORLAND GAZETTE
(WESTMINSTER PRESS LTD.)

PRINTED AND PUBLISHED BY
WESTMORLAND GAZETTE
(WESTMINSTER PRESS LTD.)
KENDAL . ENGLAND

ACKNOWLEDGMENTS

THE chapter entitled *Wordsworth in Easedale* first appeared as an article in *Ariel* and is reproduced here by kind permission of the Editor. *The Last Earl of Derwentwater* is expanded from a lecture given to the Penrith Branch of the Cumberland and Westmorland Archaeological and Antiquarian Society.

I am very grateful to Geoffrey Berry for the very excellent photographs which he has supplied by way of illustrations for this book.

Hill Top, Sawrey

LAKE COUNTRY ECHOES

CONTENTS

LIST OF ILLUSTRATIONS

INTRODUCTION

NOT the least of the various pleasures which increase the interest of a holiday in a region of strong individuality is the discovery of some of its local lore—its legends, folk tales, unusual characters, and sites and buildings of special significance.

The English Lake Country is undeniably a locality with very marked characteristics of its own. Besides being an area of supreme natural beauty, it is rich in legend, quaint superstitions, ancient customs and traditions. It has a wealth of unusual natural features as well as of sites, historic and prehistoric, where strange things have, or are reputed to have, happened.

Again, the Cumbrian people—whether they belong to Cumberland, Westmorland or Lancashire-north-of-the-Sands—can claim an ancestry of several separate strands. They have inherited, to a lesser or greater degree, something of the poetic imagination and superstition of the Celts—the Cymri, after whom their region is named; of the vigour, endurance and tenacity of the Norse Vikings who in the 9th and 10th centuries A.D., invaded Cumbria from the sea and made their homes in its scantily populated dales (Norse, dalr=a valley); and of the sober practicality of the Anglo-Saxons who at various periods, infiltrated into the district and inter-married with its inhabitants.

Above all, perhaps, they exhibit all the characteristic frugality, independence and self-sufficiency of a mountain people who for centuries were virtually detached from the life of Britain beyond the dales, and were largely dependent upon their own resources for the necessities and the relaxations of life.

All of these circumstances have combined to produce a people and an area which, even in these times of almost universal standardisation, have largely contrived to preserve an ethos and an outlook which is intriguingly and distinctively their own. This is what helps to make a Lakeland holiday markedly different from any other. In the pages which follow the visitor's attention is drawn to some of the unusual people, places and past events which contribute considerably to the area's fascination and which can add so much more interest to a vacation spent exploring some of its less obvious and less publicised charms.

This book has been written very largely with the interests of visitors to the Lake District in mind. But it is hoped that, at the same time, it may appeal to many who live in the area and may be familiar with some at least of the places mentioned, though not always, perhaps, with the stories that lie behind them.

One would like to think that it gave pleasure, also, to some who, unhappily, can enjoy the delights of Lakeland only from afar—through the medium of pictures and the printed word.

H.A.L.R.

Kirkby Lonsdale, 1973.

A VISIT TO HILL TOP

BEATRIX Potter may not have been the greatest of the many literary figures connected with the English Lake Country, but, next to the mighty Wordsworth, she could probably have claimed to be the most widely known. From the first appearance of Peter Rabbit in 1901, her stories have continued to delight successive generations of children, not only in this country but in the United States and in the several European lands into whose languages they have been translated.* Although most of these stories were written before the first World War, they still sell steadily. Their appeal is timeless, universal. Many are the shops in Lakeland which display for sale, not only the Beatrix Potter miniature classics, with their exquisitely delicate illustrations drawn by the author herself, but also figurines of the characters she created, "familiar in our mouths as household words"—Jemima Puddleduck, Pigling Bland, Tom Kitten, Mrs. Tiggy-Winkle, Hunca-Munca, and the rest of that immortal company.

It is just this perennial and wide-spread appeal of the Potter stories which helps to bestow upon Hill Top Farm, Sawrey, its peculiarly endearing quality and a charm which one can seek for in vain at many a literary shrine of greater fame and pretension.

The Beatrix Potter story is well-known, having been so admirably told by Miss Margaret Lane,† but a brief outline of her unusual career may not here be out of place. Born in London in 1866, of wealthy, middle-class parents, her childhood in a large, depressing Kensington house was mainly one of restriction and boredom. Taught by a succession of governesses, never sent to school or permitted to mix with other children, it is small wonder that Beatrix grew up shy, reserved and highly introverted. Her one outlet lay in the compan-

---

*And now, of course, the delightful film made by the Royal Ballet Company of Covent Garden has added immeasurably to the interest shown in Beatrix Potter and her immortal creations.

†*The Tale of Beatrix Potter* by Margaret Lane (Frederick Warne & Co. Ltd., 1946). A shorter account of Miss Potter appears in the present author's *Lake Country Portraits* (Harvill Press), 1967.

ionship of such pets as she was permitted or contrived to keep in the nursery of her stuffy Kensington home, and in the wild life which she and her only brother delighted to discover and study during their annual summer holidays. These were no casual affairs of a hurried fortnight or so at Eastbourne or on the Costa Brava, but family migrations, complete with domestic staff and immense quantities of luggage, to some rented furnished house in the West of England, Scotland or, in later years, the Lakes.

It was here, in Lakeland, that the young Beatrix Potter really found herself. For several summers her parents rented Wray Castle, a Victorian pseudo-baronial mansion on the shores of Windermere. Here she was free to roam the fields and woods and fell-sides; to observe closely the small creatures of woodland, hedgerow, stream and farmyard; and to make those exquisite small drawings and paintings of them in the sketch books which invariably she had with her. Here in Lakeland, she left her heart and swore life-long allegiance.

Her first attempt at writing took the form of a series of letters to a sick child, telling of the highly imaginative adventures of her pet rabbit Peter and illustrated in the margins with her own amusing sketches. There were so many of these letters that the idea occurred to her of making a short book of them for children. So was born *The Tale of Peter Rabbit*, the forerunner of the famous Potter series. First submitted to and rejected by the publishing firm of Frederick Warne, then privately printed at her own expense and sold to friends and relations, the book was ultimately re-submitted to Warnes and accepted by them. It proved magnificently successful, and from the proceeds of its sales Miss Potter was able to purchase Hill Top Farm, Sawrey, only two or three miles from Wray Castle.

Hill Top was a small and typical Westmorland farm, with all those old-fashioned features—deep sash windows, stone flag floors, black-leaded cooking range, oak panelling and staircase—in which she delighted. These features so endeared themselves to her that she determined that, so far as she could ensure it, they should never be altered or removed. Beatrix was never able to live at Hill Top; her parents were still alive and demanded her almost constant attendance. But she could and did use it as her holiday retreat, writing there many of her much-loved stories, creating those immortal characters and frequently giving them illustrations for which the farmhouse, its surroundings, the village of Sawrey and the lovely local scenery provided the perfect setting.

The farm itself she entrusted to the care of a resident manager, building an extension to one end of the original house, fully in keeping, to accommodate him and his family. Inside, the house was left unaltered, apart from the addition of items of old-fashioned furniture purchased by Beatrix at local sales and an ever-increasing collection of her own most treasured personal possessions, most of which—books, drawings, dolls' house, ornaments, etc.—are still to be seen at Hill Top today.

* * * *

There are two Sawreys—Near Sawrey, where Hill Top Farm is, is the one nearest to Hawkshead, while Far Sawrey, on the way to the Ferry across Windermere, is the one furthest from Hawkshead. Both are small, even by Lakeland village standards, and Far Sawrey in fact is little more than a hamlet. Neither, perhaps, would lay claim to spectacular beauty yet each, set in the midst of pleasant pastoral scenery, has its own quiet charm. Neither has been very much marred by new building or unmannerly modernisation and, provided one can shut one's eyes to the stream of motorised traffic, especially during the summer months, one can gaze upon virtually the scenes which so enchanted the young Beatrix Potter seventy years ago. The ancient farmsteads, whitewashed cottages, their gardens gay in summer with multi-coloured blooms, the green fields and friendly guardian fells—these remain to provide a fitting background to the shrine at Hill Top. And, since Beatrix Potter loved to draw her animal characters against a local setting, the *aficionado* will joyfully recognize many a cherished spot long familiar from the illustrations.

The very pathway leading from the road to the front entrance of Hill Top appears in *The Tale of Pigling Bland*, the front door of the farmhouse is immediately recognizable as that through which Mrs. Ribby called to borrow some yeast in *The Tale of Samuel Whiskers*, while the old oak dresser beloved of Aunt Maria, the fine oak staircase and the grandfather clock on the landing must have caused many a small visitor to look half-expectantly for a fleeting glimpse of Mrs. Tabitha Twitchit, Tom Kitten or Samuel Whiskers and the rolling pin.

Outside, in garden and farmyard, perhaps it is of Jemima Puddle-duck, so foolishly wayward and so lovable that the visitor is at once reminded. There, surely, is the actual gate through which Jemima, in poke bonnet and shawl, set off to find a suitable place among the rhubarb to lay her eggs, and beyond the farmyard the field she must cross on her way to the woods, with the glimpse of Esthwaite Water between the trees. It is no small part of the fascination of the Potter books that so many of their characters, unlike those of most children's books, are set against authentic real-life scenery. Yet how many of their young devotees, one wonders, who have not been fortunate enough to visit Hill Top, have contentedly accepted the backgrounds as being, like the characters, the product of the author's imaginative flair rather than of that side of her artistic ability which consisted in getting on to paper what she actually saw about her.

Older visitors to Hill Top, just as surely as the children, will find plenty to enchant and fascinate them, not only in the house itself and its surroundings, but also in the multitude of objects still *in situ* precisely where Beatrix Potter herself had placed them and where she stipulated in her will they should remain. For when she died it was learned that she had bequeathed Hill Top and its contents to the National Trust so that the general public, and not least those whose childhood had been gladdened by her books, could come and gaze upon the place and possessions which had given her so great a pleasure and played no small part in the bringing into existence of the books themselves.

The furniture is much as she left it—chairs, tables, dresser, rag rug, chests of drawers, four-poster bed. The family Bible still lies upon its appointed table. The French dolls are there, in their formal silken gowns, and so are the pieces of china, carefully chosen and collected and lovingly preserved. There are exquisite examples of Miss Potter's delicate, closely-observed portraiture; manuscript pages and original drawings for some of the famous books; photographs of and letters from the children for whose entertainment some of the earlier books were written—all these are among the many

small treasures preserved in this house of charm from which, to one visitor at least, the gently ironic spirit of its former possessor is never very far away.

I have talked with people who lived in or close to Sawrey and knew Beatrix Potter in her latter years. More than one of them has told me that she never really liked children and discouraged their approaches. This I find very difficult to accept. The infinite trouble she took in earlier years in seeking to cheer up sick children and to relieve the *ennui* of their temporary inactivity indicates the opposite. And so does the deep and sympathetic understanding of the child mind shown in the shape and size and presentation of the books themselves. Children's books, when Beatrix Potter began to write, tended to be large and heavy for small hands to hold. Too many of their pages presented line after line of solid unbroken letterpress, and not all their illustrators possessed the talent and charm of a Kate Greenaway, a Randolph Caldecott or a Louis Wain. And so she insisted upon small, manageable books of not much more than 5 in. × 4 in., with only a few words of text on each page and each page of text alternating with an appropriate illustration.

Although she was never able to make it her permanent home, Beatrix Potter spent what were almost certainly her happiest hours at Hill Top. She loved its peaceful unpretentiousness, the privacy which it afforded her reserved and contemplative nature, the homely routine of the adjoining farmyard, the old-fashioned flower garden which she stocked and tended in her own informal way, and the views it offered of orchard blossom in spring-time and of green fields gently rising to meet the woodland copse. She loved to pass there the hours of leisured freedom left to her after her filial duties had been performed. It was her personal sanctuary, the source of whatever she needed by way of inspiration and re-creation. Even when, in 1913, she finally asserted herself and married William Heelis, the Hawkshead solicitor who had handled the legal business of the purchase of the farm, she retained her ownership of Hill Top.

Neither Beatrix nor her quiet, middle-aged husband, however, felt that it would be suitable as the residence of a married couple, and they bought and settled down at Castle Cottage only a few hundred yards away. And since the fields which went with the cottage ran down to the roadway, with a gate almost opposite that of Hill Top, she

St. Anthony's chapel, Cartmel Fell

was frequently to be seen, clad in any old clothes which came to hand and a stout pair of locally-made clogs upon her feet, making her way across the meadows for yet another blissful sojourn in those beloved surroundings.

With Mrs. Heelis, the solicitor's wife, successful farmer and breeder of Herdwick sheep, we are not here concerned. In her later years, as a result of her long-nurtured ambitions, she became a prominent figure in agricultural and sheep-breeding circles far beyond the pleasant boundaries of Sawrey.

But her claim to whatever modest fame is rightly hers is bound up with her books, and her books, of course, are bound up with Hill Top. When she died, in 1943, among the four thousand acres of Lake Country property which it was found she had left to the National Trust, was her first and most cherished purchase itself. Still virtually as she left it, Hill Top is visited during the summer months by thousands* every year, and few of those brought up in childhood on Beatrix Potter's books can fail to be moved by its homely charm and grateful for the part it played in giving those books for the delight of so many.

---

*By sixty thousand visitors in 1971.

BELTED WILL

I ONCE spent the better part of a morning looking for Naworth Castle and saw never a glimpse of it. Yet I am assured, by people whose word I would not question, that it stands where it has stood for centuries, some dozen miles or so north-east of Carlisle and not so far from the Roman Wall. It is, of course, the seat of the Earl of Carlisle.

Like Greystoke, Naworth is one of the great houses which once belonged to the all-powerful family of Dacre and then passed into possession of the Howards as a result of the astute matrimonial dispositions made by the fourth Duke of Norfolk on behalf of his three sons. It may, perhaps, be remembered that, conveniently enough, the Duke was also guardian to the three young heiresses, all Dacres, of Dacre, Gilsland and Greystoke. What, then, more suitable than that the three young girls with great possessions but in need of husbands should be tidily disposed of in marriage to the three eligible Howard lordlings? So it came about, in 1569, that the ducal family of Howard became one of the most powerful in the North, possibly in all Elizabethan England.

Naworth is a corruption of New-Ward, itself a variant of New Castle. It was in 1313 that Ranulf de Dacre married Margaret de Multon, heiress of the barony of Gilsland, having abducted her forcibly from the custody of the Earl of Warwick, her guardian. It is some indication of the power of the Dacres at this time that no attempt was made to compel Ranulf to restore his bride to the Earl's protection, and a further indication that twenty-two years later he was granted the royal licence to crenellate. This means to build a fortified stronghold with keep, moat, curtain walls and all the other defensive apparatus of a mediaeval fortress. And so Naworth Castle sprang up on rising ground in the angle of two confluent streams, the third side of the triangle thus formed being provided with a moat.

There was abundant reason for Lord Dacre's being given permission to erect his "New Ward" so near to the Debatable Lands between England and Scotland. Bruce's victory at Bannockburn and his subsequent violent incursions south of the Border made it highly essential that the northern areas of England should be protected by as many such strongholds as possible. Dacres first, and Howards later, as Wardens of the Marches, found Naworth a very suitable base from which to conduct their defensive operations.

To return now to the Lord William Howard who, in 1569 and at the behest of the Duke his father, married Elizabeth Dacre, owner of Naworth and heiress of the Gilsland barony. It is not to be thought that Elizabeth and her husband were able to succeed to the inheritance unchallenged. Elizabeth had an uncle, Leonard Dacre, who considered himself to be the rightful heir and contested his niece's claim. A tremendous rumpus ensued, with a Commission being appointed to adjudicate upon the matter and the Queen hovering on the sidelines in the hope that some legal loop-hole might result in the estates being declared forfeit to the Crown. No such loop-hole was discovered, however. The Commission declared in favour of the Howards, and the Queen had to content herself with extorting a fine of £10,000—on the score of her consent to the marriage never having been sought or given—before Lord William and his bride were free to enter into full enjoyment of their inheritance.

Lord William Howard has been much traduced by historians north of the Border on the quite erroneous grounds that, as Lord Warden of the Marches, "Bauld Willie"—as they called him—had treated with savage injustice sundry Scottish malefactors misfortunate enough to fall into his hands. Even Sir Walter Scott, the most fair-minded of men, appears to have fallen under the same misapprehension and in *The Lay of the Last Minstrel* depicts him, under the sobriquet of "Belted Will," as the ruthless and unremitting scourge of the moss-troopers. Typical of these legends is the story that one day, when he was deeply immersed in study, news was brought to him that his men had captured a notorious Scottish reiver and now awaited their lord's instructions as to what should be done with him. "Hang him!" Lord William is supposed to have replied, without even looking up from his book. And, so the legend goes, hanged he was.

The truth of the matter is very different. Lord William was never Warden of the Marches. The iron-fisted dealings attributed to him were, in fact, those of two of his Dacre predecessors—Sir Thomas, who commanded the English reserve force at Flodden, and his eldest son, Lord William Dacre of Greystoke and Gilsland. Both were Wardens of the Marches, both exercised their office with the utmost severity. Of Sir Thomas it is recorded that in 1525, the year of his death, he gave orders that:

> "the whole garrison with the inhabitants of the country were to meet at Howtell Swyre upon Mondaye, at iiij of the clock, aft' noons the xxix of Junij, and the said company by the suffrance of God to ride into Scotland, and to cast down the tower of Kelso Abbaye and to burne the towne; the town of Sm'lawes, the town of Ormyston, and the Mossehouse."

As for his son, Lord William Dacre, he appears to have exercised his duties as Warden of the Marches in an equally forcible manner. Under suspicion of being involved in Robert Aske's rebellion, he was summoned to Westminster to stand his trial for treason. But he was acquitted by his peers, according to Dugdale:

> "By reason that the witnesses were Scotch—men of mean condition, who were thought to be suborned, and to speak maliciously against him, in regard of his severity towards them as Warden of the Marches."

Undoubtedly, as a great landowner and magistrate, our Lord William was deeply concerned with the maintenance of law and order in an area where for so many centuries both of these desirable conditions had been absent. Undoubtedly, too, he administered justice with firmness and equity. But this is far from the portrait of a harsh, merciless tyrant handed on by his detractors. He was, in truth, a man of scholarly tastes, interested deeply in matters of an antiquarian kind, a great collector of books, happiest perhaps in the study-library situated at the top of the castle's highest tower.

Lord William lived at Naworth until just before his death in 1640, pursuing his studious habits and preserving the peace of the first two Stewart kings of England with a firm, impartial hand. By 1640, however, he was 77, a considerable age for those days, and no longer able to ride forth on military or magisterial ventures. His wife, Elizabeth Dacre, pleasingly known as "Bessie of the Braid Apron," had died in the previous year. Now, in August, came news that a Scottish Covenanting army, led by the great Montrose himself, had invaded England at Coldstream, and having defeated King Charles's forces at Newburn, had occupied Newcastle. The city had capitulated under threat of bombardment.

It was feared that the victorious Scots would now turn their attentions towards Carlisle, and since Naworth was in the direct line of their probable advance preparations were hurriedly and belatedly made to put the castle into a condition capable of resistance. At the same time, in view of the detestation in which Lord William Howard was held north of the Border, it was decided that he should retire to the comparative safety of Greystoke Castle, owned and occupied by his nephew, Thomas Howard, Earl of Arundel and Surrey. The Earl, like his uncle, was a scholar and antiquary and the two men probably had much in common. In any case, it was doubtless considered that Greystoke was sufficiently far from any feasible line of march for the invaders to trouble it, and that there Lord William would be safe. Unfortunately, the upheaval seems to have proved too much for "Belted Will," and he survived his departure from Naworth for only a very brief period.

His principal agent and man of affairs seems to have been one William Radcliffe, whose "Receipts and Disbursements on behalf of the Right Honourable the Lord William Howard" from the end of August onwards contain some interesting items. For example, against the date September 1st we find:

"(Paid) to Thos. Cragg for his charges going to
Newcastle to view the Scotts Armies .. .. xs.",
and on September 18th:
"to Andrew Pott for bringing intelligence from
Morpeth of the Scots .. ..: xs."
Further entries indicate the route of Lord William's flight to safety.
"September 22nd—To the poore—my Lord going
from Nawarde to Corbye .. .. iiijs."
(Lord William owned Corby Castle as well as Naworth.)
"September 23rd—To the poore at Corbye and by
the way to Graystock .. .. vjs.
September 26th—To Thomas Baitie, for waiting
upon the litter, 5 dayes .. .. iiijs.
October 4th—To a poore manne by my Lord .. vid."

And then, sadly:

"October 7th—For a coffine for my Lord   xiiijs. iiijd.

October 8th—To the poore in the parrish of
Graystock at my Lord's burial   ..   ..   vl.xviii d.

    do.   —To five menne for ringing the bells
in Graystock church at my Lord's burial..   ..   xxij s.

    do.   —To eight menne for taking up a
marble stone in Graystock church and making a
grave there for my Lord, and for candles   xlvijs. vjd.

October 9th—To J. Hetherton of Brampton, for
lookinge to the gates at Graystock (2 dayes) at
my Lord's burial   ..   ..   ijs. vjd.

October 10th—To old Jo Hallton for his paines
at my Lord's burial..   ..   ..   vs.

October 11th—To Mr. Morland, Person of
Graystock, for a gratitude (gratuity) at my Lord's
burial..   ..   ..   xl s."

*   *   *   *

There is no record of Lord William's burial in the Greystoke church registers, but this not perhaps surprising. The keeping of registers at this date was not a matter over which any very great care was exercised. The entries, for instance, which cover the period from January 1634 to November 1644 are most confused and imperfect. They are all contained on one page, and it seems likely that the original register for these years was lost. The ancient volume which purports to record the years from 1559 to 1645 is a composite collection of entries, compiled at various times and bound up together at some date much later than the last entry.

Tradition asserts that Lord William Howard died at Thornthwaite, presumably as he was being borne on his litter towards Greystoke and safety. There is a certain bitter irony in the thought that the erstwhile "Bauld Willie" should thus have ended his colourful career as a fugitive from the foes he had defied and dominated so long.

CARTMEL FELL CHAPEL

TUCKED away in a fold of the fells between the Lyth Valley and the south-eastern end of Windermere is the only church in Lakeland dedicated to St. Anthony, the 3rd century desert-dwelling hermit. It is, perhaps, a somewhat unexpected ascription to find here, on the wooded fells above the rich, well-watered, damson-growing vale of Winster. For St. Anthony lived his long life of, reputedly, 105 years among the sun-parched sands of Egypt—healthy enough surroundings, evidently, but could the contrast be very much greater? Perhaps it was his very longevity which commended this particular saint to the men who built and hallowed, about the year 1504, the little, low-roofed chapel which bears his name.

To find the Chapel one may travel westwards from Kendal to Bowland Bridge, and then on in the same direction until the road begins its formidable ascent of Strawberry Bank. Before the most arduous gradient and the acute "hair-pin" bend are encountered, a sign-posted road forks left by way of the ancient farmstead known as Hodge Hill. From this road, about a mile along, another left fork drops sharply "down bank," as they say hereabouts, for a hundred yards or so until a further sign-post and a third left fork direct the searcher along the final short lap of his pilgrimage.

This brief thoroughfare soon peters out on a grassy plateau, punctuated by rocky outcrops and offering splendid views across the valley eastwards towards the limestone length of Whitbarrow Scar. On the fringe of this pleasant greensward the village school* flanks the lych-gate leading into the downward-sloping churchyard. This lych-gate was erected as a memorial to men of the parish who died for their country in the first World War. Before entering the chapel the visitor should note the stone mounting-block with a wooden post arising from its midst. In pre-combustion engine times such an amenity would be as acceptable to worshippers as a car park can

---

*Closed, alas, in the summer of 1971.

be today. It is fascinating to cast one's mind back over the more than four and a half centuries during which the chapel has stood and to ponder the successive generations of church-going yeomen from surrounding farmsteads and cottages who have dismounted themselves and their pillion-riding wives on these well-worn stones, casting their horses' bridles over the wooden post to prevent the animals from straying while their masters were at their devotions.

A glance at the building from the churchyard which slopes gently down towards it reveals low rough-cast walls pierced with rectangular, stone-mullioned Perpendicular windows and supporting a stone-slabbed roof of moderate pitch. At its western end is a low, gabled bell tower containing two bells, one of which is dated 1734. There is a "lean-to" vestry on the tower's northern side, while on the southern side of the main structure a deep-set porch provides access to the church—the "Browhead Chapel," incidentally, of Mrs. Humphry Ward's novel with a local setting, *Helbeck of Bannisdale*.

The interior of St. Anthony's Chapel somehow escaped the attentions of the Victorian "restorers," and consequently looks very much as it must have done at almost any time since the 17th century church reforms initiated under Archbishop Laud. There is a wealth of ancient oak, a "three-decker" pulpit dated 1698, and some capacious, fenced-in pews, with doors and screens to ensure a measure of privacy for the devotions of their occupants. The largest of these is pre-Reformation and was originally a chantry chapel, containing then the tomb of whoever endowed it and an altar at which requiem masses would be said for the repose of the dead man's soul. During the Reformation period tomb and altar were removed and the chantry was turned into a family pew. The beautifully carved screen still surrounding it has long since lost almost every trace of the rich gilding and colouring which once adorned it.

During the course of the 17th and 18th centuries most of the seating in the mountain chapels of the Lake Counties was apportioned out between the various manor houses, farms and cottages they respectively served, and the more important and influential their owners, the larger and more prominent were the places they occupied in the house of God. Strictly speaking, perhaps, this should not have been so, but even in the robustly independent regions of the North distinctions were firmly drawn, almost down to modern times, between gentry, yeoman farmers ("estatesmen") and landless labourers or hinds. It should occasion no surprise, therefore, to discover in an ancient church like St. Anthony's, Cartmel Fell, that each substantial farmstead—Hodge Hill, Comer Hall, Pool Bank, Thorpinsty Hall, Burblethwaite and so on—should have its well-established lien upon one of the more capacious and consequential pews. In the days of pew rents, their occupants would be required to pay handsomely for the privilege. It is interesting to note that the Burblethwaite Hall pew was described as "all ruinous" in 1707, and that it was rebuilt in 1811. One wonders about its condition, and whether much use was made of it, throughout the intervening century. One likes to picture also the William Hutton, whose initials (with the date 1696) are carved on the door of the Thorpinsty Hall pew. One wonders what he thought of Dutch William on the throne of England, and whether he sat in his spacious pew (albeit it is the smallest of the fenced-in ones) wearing on his head one of the elaborately curled perukes of the period—a no doubt profitless but, all the same, fascinating line of speculation. One is surely able the better to appreciate any site or scene of antiquity by attempting mentally to people it with some of those who frequented it in ages past.

An intriguing and unusual feature of St. Anthony's Chapel is the amount of ancient glass which it possesses. Some of this glass, it is believed, was brought from Cartmel Priory, possibly to prevent its destruction at the hands of iconoclastic reformers.

The 15th century glass in the east window above the altar depicts St. Anthony with his customary symbols of a bell, a boar and a "T" shaped staff. The three central panels, although at some time they have suffered a certain amount of damage and fragmentation, illustrate five of the Seven Sacraments—Penance, Eucharist, Holy Unction, Marriage and Ordination. The two Sacraments of Christian Initiation—Baptism and Confirmation—are missing, and their place has been taken by the figures of St. John the Baptist and two other saints whose identity has not been established. Portraits of the donor and his wife also appear in the lower part of the window.

In the panel on the right hand of the three central lights, we see St. Leonard, patron saint of prisoners, bearing as his symbol a piece of broken chain. In this panel, also, on a plain portion of the glass, appears a grim reminder of the hazards of travel in bygone ages, some unknown hand having inscribed in paint:

"Wilm brigg goeth to London upon tusday,
xijth day of Aprill. God save hym."

And at the base of the window is inscribed in Latin:

"Pray for the souls of Miles Brigg (and of his wife . . .)
benefactors of this (church?)."

There are fragments of mediaeval glass in both the north and south windows of the chancel, the figure of the Risen Christ being plainly distinguishable in that on the north side above the pew appertaining to Comer Hall. Equally worthy of notice are the two small windows on the north side of the sanctuary. These indicate that once there were two chambers or cells adjoining the church, one above the other, probably for the use of visiting priests.* If, as is likely, the church was served for the first forty or so years of its existence from Cartmel Priory, there must have been many occasions in winter when weather conditions and the state of the roads—such as they were then—made it necessary for officiating clergy to remain at Cartmel Fell overnight. Hence the provision of a priestly "flat."

In this same corner of the church is a tombstone with an inscription, the pathos of which pervades even the stilted style in which it is written:

"Underneath this stone a mould'ring Virgin lies,
Who was the pleasure once of Human eyes.
Her blaze of charms Virtue well approv'd;
The Gay admired, much the Parents lov'd.
Transitory live, death untimely came,
Adieu, Farewell, I only leave my name."

The subject of this sad little encomium was Betty Poole, aged three years.

In addition to the pulpit and pews there are other items of 17th or 18th century woodwork, notably the former altar now used as a credence table, the altar rails, some Jacobean coffin stools and a

---

*As at Greystoke, where the two chambers still exist. The lower one is used as a vestry.

bishop's chair, bearing the date 1645, which was given to the church in 1936. More recent gifts are a picture of St. Anthony, done in what are believed to be 17th century Dutch tiles and to be seen on the south wall of the church, and a similar representation of St. Mary Magdalene, which is in the vestry—a later addition to the building.

In the vestry, also, is a carved figure of Christ, very much damaged through past ill-usage, which is said to be the original figure from the pre-Reformation Rood beam and probably the only surviving example of its kind in the country. Among other antiquities to be seen in this fascinating little church are a pewter flagon dated 1635–40, an 18th century pitch pipe and an ancient collecting box.

THE GILPINS OF KENTMERE

THE motorist heading for the Lakes from Kendal, on the main
A591 Windermere road, passes first through the small town of
Staveley which, although it was a market town as far back as the
reign of Edward III, today offers small inducement for Lakeland-
bound travellers to pause and explore. And since the sign directing
to Kentmere is sited on the right-hand extremity of a left-hand bend
in the middle of the village (for truly it is little more), it is probably
noticed by very few of them. This is a pity, for Kentmere offers a
pleasant short excursion of only three miles in each direction.

One has to say "in each direction" since the dale is a cul-de-sac
and what goes up, in the way of wheeled traffic, must come down.
For the energetic walker who objects to retracing his steps there is
a rough mountain track which leads, by way of Garburn Pass,
over into the Troutbeck Valley.

Kentmere is something of a misnomer nowadays. The dale road
keeps close for most of the way to the course of the river Kent, as it
bounds along southwards full of youthful exuberance. But the mere
which gave the dale its name was drained some hundred and fifty
years ago, and from all one has read of its boggy, reed-congested
fringes its disappearance probably cannot be reckoned as any great
tragedy. In some old books it appears as *Kentmire*.

The dale road winds pleasurably along its twisting, tree-lined
course, now on this side of the stream, now on that. For the first
mile or so, where the hills close in and the valley floor is so narrow,
river and road are seldom more than a few feet apart. Sudden shafts
of sunlight through the trees, glinting on foam-flecked waters and
spray-splashed boulders, catch the eye from time to time, threatening
to distract the motorist from watching as alertly as he should for
the next sudden swing of his route from right to left.

Presently the valley opens out, the hills withdraw themselves to a
respectful distance, the river flows more sedately and further afield
between widening meadows of lush, flower-bedecked pasture. The
diatomite factory, lurking discreetly behind its sheltering girdle of

trees and scarcely obtruding upon a scene little changed over the centuries, is soon left behind. Now a few scattered farmhouses, cottages, barns and byres pleasantly punctuate the pastoral prose. Their deep-set porches, twinkling windows and white-washed walls provide, as elsewhere in Lakeland, the perfect foil to the lush greenery of field and fell. Many of these have stood here since the 17th or 18th centuries, in company with the little stone church with its saddle-backed tower which somehow suggests Sussex rather than Westmorland—or perhaps some even remoter Continental prototype.

The 18th century school, now a youth hostel, no longer launches the children of the dale upon their lettered way. Instead, they are whisked away each morning by 'bus to Staveley—even the smallest of them—and returned each evening; tired little commuters who, on winter school-days, are absent from dawn to dusk from the small community to which they belong. No doubt they benefit educationally, if not in other ways. But something vital is wrenched from rural life when a village school is closed. It is not only the loss of youthful shouts and laughter as children are released from lessons which is to be regretted. The old village loyalty, the sense of belonging to a clearly-defined group and place in which one had one's roots and towards which one had a feeling of affection and obligation— these tend to dwindle when the local school no longer provides the background for the country child's formative years. The school 'bus and the "comprehensive" conveyor belt have doubtless done much to widen the outlook (if not to improve the manners or deepen the wisdom) of children from the remoter areas, but one can scarce suppress a sigh of regret for the fatal blows they have dealt to the life of many a now semi-deserted or semi-dormitory village or hamlet.

Towards the dale-head on the eastern side, as the high fells begin to push their lower slopes out into the valley bottom, is Millrigg, and above it are indications of man's earliest occupation hereabouts —scattered stones surrounded by a grass-grown rampart which in prehistoric times was a fortified settlement. It is well-sited, well above the miasma-laden marshes which would then cover the floor of the dale, and convenient to the mountain passes of Garburn and Nan Bield, the latter leading over into Mardale. Hidden mercifully out of sight from below, the modern reservoir has been built further still up the valley, where it can fulfil its necessary function with the least possible detriment to the beauty of the dale.

By far the most interesting, historically, of man's additions to the locality is Kentmere Hall, a semi-ruinous pele-tower flanking a farmhouse of later date. This is the ancient home of the Gilpin family, who received the lordship of Kentmere from the Barons of Kendal as far back as the reign of King John (1199–1216). The boar's head which appears as the family crest is derived, according to long tradition, from the slaying by Richard Gilpin, lord of the manor and a soldier of renown, of a ferocious wild boar which was terrorising the valley. Richard it was who adopted as the family motto the words *Dictis factisque simplex*—"Simple in speech and deed."

Perhaps the most notable member of the Gilpin family (if we except the equestrian John of Cowper's poem who, if he existed in fact, may have been a member of the clan) was Bernard, born at Kentmere Hall in 1517. His uncle had fought on the losing side at Bosworth Field and, like Richard III, had died on the field of battle. Bernard's father, who was a younger brother, then inherited the estate, married Margaret Layton of Dalemain, near Ullswater, and by her had six children of whom Bernard was the youngest.

The boy early showed signs of the piety which, after his studies at Queen's College, Oxford, led him to take Holy Orders. He came to manhood just at the time when Henry VIII was engaged in revolutionising the social and religious life of England by destroying and despoiling the monasteries, achieving thereby the double aim of spiting the Pope and filling his own pockets. As a student of divinity, young Gilpin found himself inevitably involved in the theological ferment of the time. At first he was able to summon up small enthusiasm for the new doctrines brought into the country by exiles returning from the Continent after the death of Henry. He was, however, sufficiently realistic not to doubt that moderate reform, on the lines advocated by the Dutch scholar Erasmus, was greatly needed if the English Church was to survive the impact of the New Learning. He expressed himself to this effect in correspondence with extremists in the two opposed camps, but steadily declined to subscribe to the policies and tenets of the more fanatical reformers.

Gilpin was temperamentally a "middle-of-the-road" man, and his ecclesiastical outlook was that *via media* which later was to establish itself as the characteristically Anglican position, opposed equally to

the extremes of Papist and Puritan alike.* But when the reaction
under Queen Mary set in, his moderation was not enough to save
him from suspicion. He was summoned to London to explain some
of his written and spoken statements. He travelled south guarded
by an armed escort to whom he made no secret of the fact that the
stake was all that he looked for at the journey's end. However,
providence intervened. He fell from his horse and broke his leg,
and by the time he was able to travel again Queen Mary was dead
and he was set at liberty.

Gilpin was at this time incumbent of the parish of Houghton-le-
Spring, a benefice to which he had been appointed by his kinsman,
Bishop Tunstall. Here he elected to remain for the next thirty years,
until his death at the age of sixty-six in 1583. In 1560 he was offered
the Bishopric of Carlisle, and a year or so later the Provostship of
his old *alma mater*, Queen's College, Oxford. Both of these prefer-
ments he declined. He found complete fulfilment in ministering to
his rural flock, entertaining and dispensing charity on a generous
scale. His income of £400 was a good one for those days, but since
he was unmarried and had reduced his own personal wants to the
barest minimum he gave away most of his stipend in one way or
another.

Open house was kept at Houghton Rectory, both for man and
beast. Queen Elizabeth's powerful minister, Lord Burghley, was
entertained with his entourage on such a scale that he compared
Gilpin's hospitality with what might have been looked for at
Lambeth Palace. It was a jest in the locality that if even a horse
were turned astray it would turn up before long at Houghton
Rectory.

On Sundays dinner was provided for any parishioners or visitors
to the church who cared to avail themselves of it. Every day there
was hot broth to be had by the poor of the parish, with a special
issue of meat on Thursdays. At Christmas Gilpin gave an ox to
be roasted and divided amongst them. In those days of intense
poverty among the labouring class, many of whom had been
employed by the monasteries or had received free collations of food
daily at their gates, such help as men like Gilpin gave of their
liberality must have saved many a family from starvation.

*His uncle was Bishop Tunstall of Durham, another middle-of-the-road man who
had contrived to ride the whirlwind of four tempestuous reigns.

Kentmere Hall

Nor were his benefactions confined to his own parish of Houghton. Those were times, not only of economic distress, but also of ecclesiastical disorder. There was an acute shortage of clergy and many parishes were without a resident priest. To help alleviate this lack, Gilpin undertook numerous preaching tours over a wide area of the North, recalling the neglected country folk to the claims of Christianity, baptising their babies, instructing their young, and generally seeking by his preaching and teaching to dissipate the dark ignorance in which so many were otherwise fated to pass their lives. Nor, while ministering to their spiritual needs, was the good man forgetful of their material wants. He invariably set out on his evangelistic missions with ten pounds in his purse for the relief of any distress he might encounter; and whenever he returned his purse would be empty.

Like many another Churchman of his time (such as his fellow-Northerner, Edwin Sandys, whose extreme Puritanism Gilpin abhorred), the "Apostle of the North," as he came to be known, was acutely aware of the lack of educational opportunities existing in the northern parts of the country for lads of promising ability. Many grammar schools were built and endowed throughout the country during Queen Elizabeth's reign, a great number of them as the result of the promptings and benefactions of Churchmen, clerical and lay. Gilpin was responsible for the foundation of such a school in his own neighbourhood, again devoting a generous sum from his own purse to its endowment and maintenance. Several lads of exceptional promise he sent to the University, maintaining them throughout their student years and keeping in regular touch with them by correspondence. Among those whom he helped in this way were George Carleton, who became Bishop of Chichester; Henry Ayray, who subsequently achieved the eminence which Gilpin himself had declined, becoming Provost of Queen's College, Oxford; and Hugh Broughton, who repaid his benefactor's generosity towards him by intriguing to have Gilpin removed from his living on the grounds of increasing age and himself, Broughton, appointed to succeed him. It is pleasant to record that this monstrous act of ingratitude met with the failure that it merited.

There are many stories told about this greatly loved and revered pastor, of which the best-known, perhaps, is that of the theft of his horse which he had left quietly grazing outside a house where he was visiting. When the thieves discovered whose mount they had stolen they hurriedly returned it to Houghton Rectory, saying that they knew that "any who robbed Master Gilpin would go straight to hell." This saintly priest is fittingly commemorated at Durham in the Bernard Gilpin Society, a modern, non-collegiate foundation affiliated to the University and catering for non-graduate students whose intention it is to train for Holy Orders.

Bernard's elder brother George rose high in the royal service, eventually becoming Queen Elizabeth's Ambassador to the Netherlands. But a later George, great-grandson to the diplomat, suffered severely for his loyalty to his Sovereign. He came out on the side of King Charles I in the Civil War, and when it proved to be the losing side Captain George Gilpin was forced to go into exile. He had married Catherine Philipson of Hollin Hall, and when compelled to seek refuge abroad he appointed his wife's cousin, Sir Christopher Philipson, as one of the trustees of his property. Thus, when George died in exile and without an heir Kentmere Hall and lands passed finally from the Gilpin family and (in 1660, at the Restoration) into Philipson hands.

Two descendants of the Kentmere Gilpins achieved a measure of fame in the 18th century. Sawrey Gilpin, who was born in Carlisle in 1733, became the most successful painter of horses in this country until Stubbs, and was elected President of the Royal Society of Artists in 1773. Sawrey's brother, the Rev. William Gilpin, kept a school at Cheam in Surrey and held educational theories which were considered remarkably advanced for his time. He was also an author of some repute, the best-known of his books being his *Life* of his famous ancestor Bernard (published in 1752), and his *Tour in the Mountains and Lakes of Cumberland and Westmorland*, one of the earliest (1787) of the unending stream of Lakeland Guide books.

The Reverend William's son, John Bernard Gilpin, emigrated to Massachusetts, where he founded a family several of whom have attained eminence in the public and political life of the United States. One of them became the first Governor of the newly-constituted State of Colorado. Yet another collateral descendant of the Apostle of the North, Catherine Gilpin, was born at Scaleby Castle in 1738 and in her day was accounted a poet of no small merit.

There are still Gilpins resident in the Lake Counties, many of them no doubt able to claim descent from the former lords of Kentmere. Those who visit this pleasant dale today and view the semi-ruined pele-tower adjoining the present farmhouse may perhaps be tempted to think in terms of departed grandeur. If this be so, they might profitably ponder upon the contribution made to the life of the Lake Counties over the centuries by members of this ancient family, and not least by him whose memorial tablet in Kentmere Church bears the inscription:

"A pattern parish priest, he was as saintly as he was brave, as generous as he was just, as practical as he was enthusiastic. An ardent student of Scripture, he did not undervalue the primitive tradition. An impassioned missionary, he won the name of the Apostle of the North. Refusing all honours save the honour of serving his Master, Christ, he kept a tender conscience unspotted from the world, and left behind him an imperishable name."

THE GREAT KENDAL RIOT

IN the early part of the year 1818 a parliamentary election was announced in which the electors of Kendal (householders of property worth forty shillings or more) were invited to choose between Lord Lowther, the Tory candidate, and Mr. Henry (later Lord) Brougham for the Whigs. Political feeling was running high at the time throughout the country and although in those pre-Reform Bill days only a small minority of citizens were qualified to vote, there were plenty of their fellow-townsmen who were more than prepared to help them to a right decision by vehement and frequently violent demonstrations. Election meetings were usually held in the open air, candidates and supporting speakers addressing their tumultuous audiences either from temporary platforms known as "hustings," or from the balcony or upstairs window of some convenient hostelry. And, since large quantities of free liquor would have been provided by the opposition's agents for an hour or two before the advertised time of the meeting, speakers could expect not merely a good deal of rowdy heckling but also a barrage of rotten eggs, fruit and vegetables, as well as an assortment of even more noisome projectiles.

The 1818 election in Kendal led to scenes of disorder, violence and destruction such as would make most modern students' "demos" seem tea-party tame by comparison. The whole disreputable episode is described at great length in Mr. John F. Curwen's *Kirkbie Kendall* (1900), which has long been out of print.

It would appear that on February 3rd Lord Lowther and his brother Colonel Lowther announced that they would be visiting Kendal a week or so later to solicit the support of the local electors. The town seems to have been fairly evenly divided between supporters of the "Yellow" (the Tories) and the "Blue" (the Whigs), but the situation was complicated by the presence in the town of large numbers of Irish labourers who were employed in the construction of the Kendal–Lancaster Canal. These navvies ("navigators") were probably gloriously indifferent as to which candidate was elected, but were prepared to shout indiscriminately for either side if first supplied liberally with strong drink.

The local Tory Committee had made elaborate arrangements for their candidate to be met with a band, a huge yellow banner and a detachment of the Westmorland Yeomanry, and for the ringing of the bells of the parish church. They had also, inadvisedly as it turned out, provided lavish quantities of free liquor. This provision was taken full advantage of by the populace, whatever their political preferences, the Irish labourers exhibiting no unnatural diffidence in doing likewise. The consequences were catastrophic.

With considerable astuteness, Mr. Brougham's committee had issued an appeal requesting that "Gentlemen" should comport themselves with propriety upon the occasion of Lord Lowther's visit and thus give no grounds for discredit to be cast upon "so good a cause as the glorious emancipation of Westmorland from its long thraldom to their opponents." The wily Whigs can scarcely have supposed that much heed would be taken of such a "request," and would no doubt have been deeply chagrined if it had. In the event, having thus publicly absolved themselves in advance, they had no cause to be disappointed.

On the morning of February 16th a cavalcade of Lowther supporters set out to meet the candidate and his party, who were coming from Dallam Tower, near Milnthorpe, where they had spent the night. The mob were ready. As soon as the Kendal horsemen emerged from the stable yard of the Commercial Inn they were met with volleys of mud and stones. Immediately there was pandemonium. Terrified horses reared, plunged and bolted with their bruised and bespattered riders, and only with the utmost difficulty was the cavalcade re-formed and able to set off in the direction of Milnthorpe. Here they met the Tory candidate and his entourage and, battered though they were, at once turned about for Kendal.

The procession which now approached the town consisted of eleven carriages, 131 horsemen and a detachment of dismounted yeomanry. All went well until this impressive array arrived at Nether Bridge, at the southern entrance to the town. Here they found the road barricaded with a formidable barrier of flags and paving stones, from behind which the mob once more let fly a paralysing fusillade of brickbats and refuse. Again some of the horses bolted, but others were brought under control by their

riders who at once charged the hastily erected barricades, making a
gap for Lord Lowther's carriage to pass through and momentarily
scattering the mob. Before the rest of the cavalcade could pass the
barrier, however, the rioters rallied, resumed the attack, and caused
two of the supporters' carriages to become so inextricably entangled
that the road was completely blocked for the rest of the day. Those
horsemen who had not passed the barrier were forced to retreat out
of harm's way and return whence they had come.

Meanwhile, the vanguard had run the gauntlet of their attackers
and had won through to Highgate. Here they were met by a comparatively peaceful procession of Whig supporters accompanied by a
band and two large banners, one of blue, the Whig colours, the
other a white one carrying anti-Tory slogans such as "No Corn
Bill," "No Suspension of the Habeas Corpus Act," "Brougham
for Ever" and "Liberty of the Press." Courteously the Whigs divided
their ranks, so forming two columns for Lord Lowther and his
friends to pass between, the two banners dipped at the end of it to
form a mock triumphal arch.

This was clearly more than Tory pride could be expected to
stomach. Before anyone could guess his intent, the horseman who
bore the yellow Lowther standard galloped forward, seized both
blue and white flags from their astonished guardians and rode
triumphantly off with all three ensigns. Again chaos broke loose.
Horses once more became unmanageable, political opponents fell to
fighting, and Lord Lowther with some of his followers took refuge
in the *King's Arms*, the Colonel and others in the *Commercial Inn*.
As the Lowther carriage, already sadly battered, drew up at the door
of the *Commercial*, it received renewed onslaughts from the Irish
navvies, who wrenched off its doors and slashed its upholstery.

Meanwhile the intrepid Tory standard bearer, with his trophies,
had found refuge within the *King's Arms*, closely pursued by a hostile
crowd which threatened to demolish the old inn stone by stone
unless the Whig banners were handed back. Only when this was done
was the attack on the hostelry called off. Now it was the turn of
the *Commercial* to attract the attention of the rioters. Here the
navvies broke into the inn kitchen, seizing and devouring the
freshly-roasted round of beef about to be served up for the delect-

ation of the inn's patrons. Only by offering each man a free pint of ale to go to the *White Hart* did the innkeeper rid himself of his voracious and unwelcome guests.

Off to the *White Hart* lurched the drink-inflamed Irish, there to repeat their behaviour at the *Commercial*, eating and drinking all that they could get at, and smashing up furniture and fixtures. This wholesale mayhem, of course, attracted envious attention from the local ruffians who proceeded to fight their way into the inn and, after a Homeric battle, to evict the Irishmen. By the time that both groups had finished with it, the *White Hart* had been more or less gutted.

At the *Commercial Inn*, whence the tide of conflict had now receded, Lord Lowther and his party were able to bathe their wounds, clean up their battle-stained costumes and refresh themselves with such food and drink as had escaped the voracity of the fierce Hibernians. Later, however, when they attempted to harangue the populace from the windows of the inn, a renewed onslaught was made, in which windows were smashed, doors battered down and the would-be representative of this turbulent town was forced to flee with his friends by way of the inn's rear premises.

Then the winter evening descended, and with the darkness Kendal's "Donnybrook" was brought mercifully to an end.

SIR JOHN BARROW

TRAVELLERS approaching the small town of Ulverston by way of the A590 road from Newby Bridge are confronted, just before they reach the town, with a grassy, cone-shaped hill surmounted by what looks like the Eddystone Lighthouse. It is, in fact, a replica of Smeaton's famous beacon tower, built in this case not to give warning to ships at sea but to commemorate one of Ulverston's most distinguished sons.

John Barrow was born at near-by Dragley Beck, in a cottage which still stands, on June 19th, 1764. His father, Roger Barrow, was a smallholder who had migrated some years before from Patterdale. His mother, born Mary Dawson, was a local woman. Such were the humble beginnings of one who was to hold for most of his life a position of high importance and responsibility in the Civil Service and who, for the greater part of his career, was to move on terms of easy familiarity in the most exalted circles.

Young Barrow showed from an early age signs of unusual abilities and was sent to Ulverston Grammar School. Here the Headmaster was the Reverend William Tyson Walker, son of the legendary "Wonderful Walker" of Seathwaite and a good classical scholar. As was the custom in the country grammar schools of those days, the boys at Ulverston were given a good grounding in Greek and Latin language and literature, with a fair smattering of Shakespeare thrown in for good measure. Judged by modern educational standards, it was perhaps an austere academic diet but, by familiarising the young with the culture of the ancient world and with some of the greatest works of literature of all time, such a curriculum imparted to those who were exposed to it a high degree of cultivation as well as an ability to express themselves in speech and writing with a facility and precision none too common among the products of our modern technologically biased systems.

Unlike Wordsworth, who was a few years his junior, John Barrow was not able to proceed from North Country grammar school to university. The straitened circumstances of his parents made it imperative for him to leave school, and to earn some

money at the early age of thirteen. So he embarked upon a succession
of jobs, each of which in some way or another seems to have made
a significant contribution to the lad's store of knowledge and
abilities. His first employment was as assistant to a local surveyor,
and in this capacity, no doubt, young Barrow's mental alertness
and eagerness to learn enabled him to assimilate a fresh range of
skills and information.

Surveying, however, does not seem to have detained him long for
we next find him, while still only fourteen, acting as tutor to a young
midshipman who was actually a year or two older than himself!
Indeed it seems to have been a question at times of who was tutor
and who was the pupil, for from his protégé Barrow is said to have
learned the elements of navigation. At this stage the boy seems to
have felt drawn to a life at sea, understandably perhaps in view of
the fact that he had spent the whole of his life so far within sight
and sound of it. It was perhaps with a seafaring career in mind
that he now took some lessons in advanced mathematics from an
eccentric recluse who lived on the fringes of the Lake District.

Soon, however, he is seen flexing his wings for further flight, this
time to as far away as Liverpool, where a chance acquaintance had told
him there was a job to be had as book-keeper in a small iron foundry.
Here young John lived with his employer's family, and here he
had his first glimpses of the great world beyond the somewhat
circumscribed limits of North Lonsdale.* Here he saw the celebrated
Mrs. Siddons perform, though in what part history does not relate.
And here, too, he saw the aeronaut Lunardi make one of the earliest
balloon ascents in Britain.

Then, quite suddenly, the owner of the foundry died and young
Barrow found himself once more seeking employment. Again
through the good offices of a friend, something turned up at the
appropriate moment. There was a vacancy for a deck-hand on a
Greenland whaler which was just about to set off for a summer's
fishing in Arctic waters. Barrow was offered the job and eagerly
signed on. The whaler spent the summer months cruising and
hunting off Spitzbergen, and so was formed an acquaintance with
those frozen Northern wastes which were to occupy so large a place
in his thoughts in later years.

---

*i.e., Lancashire north of Morecambe Bay.

When at the end of the season the whaler returned to Liverpool and discharged her crew, young John was once more faced with the problems of unemployment. Once again good fortune, allied to his own abundant energy and self-confidence, came to his aid. He was told of a school at Greenwich kept by a Dr. James, who was in need, it appeared, of a tutor to teach mathematics. It was a school of some standing, numbering among its former pupils James Wolfe, the conqueror of Quebec, and John Jervis, the future Admiral who became Earl St. Vincent. Unabashed by the school's prestige or by his own slender experience and qualifications, Barrow set out for London, was interviewed by Dr. James and engaged for a period of three years. Never again was he to return to his native North Country.

At Greenwich Barrow was able to join in a variety of local activities. There, of course, was the great Naval Hospital, founded in the reign of William III on the site of the former royal palace; there was a Nautical School, which trained lads for the lower decks of His Majesty's ships; and there was the Royal Observatory. All of these activities attracted to the neighbourhood numerous residents of education and ability, who provided a lively social background to Greenwich's more serious concerns. All this young Barrow found highly congenial and he was quick to acquire an acquaintance-ship which once more was to help to further his career. This is not to imply that he deliberately cultivated only those whom he considered might be of use to him. It was natural that he should be attracted to those whose interests he shared, and most of the friendships he made in this way appear to have been of long endurance.

Among those whom he met and who became a firm friend, was Sir George Staunton, who asked Barrow to tutor his son Thomas. Once again it might seem to be a question of which was the teacher and which the taught, for at the age of twelve young Thomas, a highly intelligent and indeed precocious youngster, could already converse in five languages, among them Chinese. From his remark-able pupil Barrow only less remarkably picked up a working know-ledge of Mandarin, so that when Sir George Staunton's close friend Lord Macartney was sent out as Britain's first Ambassador to China in 1792, not only was young Thomas taken as His Excellency's page but John Barrow was chosen to be Comptroller of the Ambassa-dor's household. Diplomatically and politically the Mission was not an unqualified success, but Barrow, with his active inquiring mind, enjoyed himself greatly. A few years later, in 1806, he wrote and published an account of all that he had been able to observe and record of a country then virtually unknown to more than a handful of "foreign devils." The title of the book was *Travels in China*, and it marked a notable step in Barrow's progress in the world of public affairs.

Before his book on China appeared, however, Barrow had been adding to his store of geographical knowledge elsewhere. In 1796 Lord Macartney was appointed first Governor-General of Cape Colony, recently taken from the Dutch to prevent its falling into the hands of Napoleon and so menacing the sea routes to India vital to a Britain engaged in a life or death struggle with revolutionary France. Once more Macartney took Barrow with him, this time as private secretary. And once more the young man's lively curiosity and powers of observation were brought into use in studying the botany and geology of southernmost Africa. They were employed too in taking careful note of the problems created by Boer farmers who chafed at any attempt at legislative control from Cape Town; by the pressures put upon the expanding colony by encroaching Bantu tribes pressing steadily southwards from central Africa; and by the process of extermination which the aboriginal inhabitants of the Cape—Hottentots and primitive "Stone Age" type Bushmen—were undergoing at the hands of Boer and Bantu alike.

Barrow was employed by the Governor-General in numerous tasks of a pacifying or fact-finding nature, smoothing over the angry complaints of up-country settlers at bureaucratic interferences from the Cape and especially at the way their handling of the natives was criticised and controlled by Government regulations. When he went up to Graaf Reinet Barrow found the Boer farmers in a state of incipient revolt, and only by the exercise of considerable tact was he able to soothe their embittered feelings. He also exhibited no small skill in his handling of the native tribes and their leaders. Exploring beyond the Great Fish River, he met Gaika, the formidable chief of the war-like Xosas, and in the north-western areas of Cape Colony he saw something of the already diminishing Bushmen and Hottentots. Once more he made copious notes of all that he was able to observe and when, after his return to England, he published the results in his *Travels in the Interior of Southern Africa* he pro-

vided what was the first factual and accurate account of the hinterland
and tribal areas.

Lord Macartney resigned in November, 1798 on account of ill-
health, but Barrow remained behind at the Cape, as secretary to
General Dundas, the Deputy Governor. Once again trouble flared
up among the Boers at Graaf Reinet over the Cape Government's
inability to halt the infiltration of the Bantu from the east, and over
their refusal to allow the Boers to take matters into their own hands.
And once more Barrow was sent to deal with the situation, again
successfully. Then, in January 1802, came news of the abortive
Treaty of Amiens, the British flag was hauled down at the Cape, and
the Colony was handed back to the Dutch. Barrow was one of the
last of the British officials to leave.

Back in London, he found that Lord Macartney had reported
enthusiastically on his (Barrow's) work in South Africa, and before
long he was offered the important post of Second Secretary to the
Admiralty. Eagerly he accepted the post, one which he was to hold,
with only a short break, until his retirement forty-one years later.

Barrow came to the Admiralty at a critical moment in the affairs
of Britain and of the British Navy. War was resumed with Revolutionary France early that year, and Nelson's decisive victory at
Trafalgar was only a matter of months away in the future. Meanwhile
there was much to be done to bring Admiralty administration and
organization up-to-date. At that time there was a Board of Admiralty
which controlled, as far as possible in the circumstances of the time,
the movements and staffing of ships; a Navy Board which handled
supplies, equipment, repairs, etc.; and sundry committees dealing
with various other branches of the Service. Each separate body had
its own independent board of control, and was housed apart in its
own premises. The delays, confusion and wastage resulting from this
inept arrangement were incalculable. It was one of Barrow's major
achievements during his time at the Admiralty that he was able to
exert pressure and initiate the reforms which were to bring this state
of things to an end. To him, more than to any other single person,
must be given the credit for bringing all Naval administration under
the control of the one Board of Admiralty and for speeding up
Admiralty procedure generally. Many of these changes he was able
to press for successfully during the time that his fellow-Cumbrian,

Sir James Graham, was at the Admiralty as First Lord. Barrow has deservedly been described as the greatest Secretary to the Navy since Samuel Pepys, and the baronetcy which he received in 1835 was a fitting reward for his services.

After Waterloo, with so many naval ships and crews available for peaceful employment, Barrow's thoughts turned to Arctic exploration and in particular to the problem of finding a north-west passage into the Pacific. Ever since his whaling trip to Spitzbergen this fascinating possibility had been present in his mind. Now he began to urge upon the Government not only the practicability but also the commercial and strategic advantages of a clear-water passage from ocean to ocean if such existed. As a result of his friendship with Sir Joseph Banks, the eminent naturalist who had accompanied Captain Cook on his voyages, Barrow had been elected a Fellow of the Royal Society in 1806 and he was also to be one of the founders of the Royal Geographical Society in 1830. Now his powerful advocacy, backed by the veteran Banks, led to the sending of successive expeditions under Ross and Parry into the dark, inhospitable Arctic waters. None of these was successful in penetrating into the Pacific, but much invaluable knowledge was gained. Barrow's part in the initiating and despatching of the expeditions was given permanent recognition by the naming after him of an island and a strait in the Arctic Sea. The final, tragic expedition of Sir John Franklin, of which there were no survivors, set out in 1845.

At Sir Joseph Banks's house in Soho Square, Barrow met on terms of close friendship many of the leading men of science of the day; men such as Maskelyne, the Astronomer Royal, Sir Humphry Davy and Sir John Rennie. He was in the chair at a meeting on May 24th, 1830, when it was decided to promote "the Geographical Society of London," later to become the Royal Geographical Society, and was elected Vice-President. He wrote the first article for the *Geographical Journal*, and over the years was to contribute no fewer than 195 articles for this periodical, most of them dealing with travel, exploration, discovery, natural history or naval reform. Among his other writings were biographies of Admirals Lord Anson and Lord Howe, and an account of the *Mutiny on the Bounty* which is still in print in the "World's Classics" series of the Oxford University Press.

Sir John Barrow retired from the Admiralty in 1845, having been Secretary for over forty years. He was eighty-one, and nowadays would probably have enjoyed twenty years of retirement on a comfortable pension. He died on November 23rd, 1848, and was buried in the churchyard of All Saints' parish church, Camden Town, where a marble obelisk marks his grave.

Although, so far as is known, he had never returned to his birthplace near the shores of Morecambe Bay, the people of Ulverston did not forget to pay tribute to their illustrious fellow-townsman. The cost of the tower erected to his memory on the Hill of Hoad was subscribed to by the Queen Dowager (Queen Adelaide), Lord Palmerston and a number of eminent naval men, and when the foundation stone was laid, on a May day in 1850, the ceremony was attended by more than eight thousand people. Thus is a Lancashire hill-top linked with a barren island and the icy waters of a strait in the Arctic Circle in its homage to a local lad who played no small part in the establishing of Britain's maritime greatness in 19th century war and peace.

IN AND AROUND CLAPPERSGATE

THE visitor leaving the main Lakeland artery—the Windermere–Keswick road—on his way to Skelwith Bridge, the Langdales, Coniston, Hawkshead and the Sawreys, must needs pass through the small hamlet of Clappersgate and its attendant cluster of houses across the river Brathay. Speeding along the widened highway, pressed perhaps for time, he may retain no more than a fleeting impression of some personable Lake Country cottages washed in agreeable shades of white, cream, ochre and pink. He may even catch a glimpse of a few larger houses lurking shyly behind screening shrubs and evergreens; and of the river Brathay rushing beneath the ancient bridge *en route* for its brief rendezvous with the Rothay, before their combined identity is lost almost at once in the majestic embrace of Windermere.

Yet there is more to Clappersgate/Brathay than a huddle of habitations nervously flanking a much frequented highway. Clappersgate has a past of some antiquity and considerable interest. Situated near the confluence of the Brathay and Rothay rivers, and at the junction of trackways which later grew into roads of importance, its position alone would account for its existence.

The meaning and origin of the name have long been debated. "Gate" in the Norse tongue from which so many Cumbrian place-names are derived usually means a "track-way" or road, while the first part of the name is believed by scholars to mean "stepping-stones." Wherever one comes across an ancient stone bridge it is usually safe to assume that it took the place of an earlier wooden one, and wooden bridges not infrequently were erected where there was a "wath" or ford, or where stepping-stones provided a river crossing-place—except, of course, when the river was in spate. It is possible, then, that the name "Clappersgate" indicates the linking of two important trackways by stepping-stones across the Brathay.

The hamlet is but a mile or so westwards of Borrans, at the northern end of Windermere, where stood the Roman fort of Galava. This was a staging post between the main north–south military route from Lancaster to the Wall, and the westward line of march, across the fells by way of Wrynose and Hardknott, to Ravenglass and the sea. Clappersgate must often have watched the columns of mercenaries picking their way painfully along its stony tracks.

Centuries later, this strategic junction and crossing place gained a new importance as the Augustinian Canons of Conishead Priory acquired land in the neighbourhood. They would come by way of Newby Bridge and Hawkshead to collect their rents, arrange for the sale of beasts and wool, and generally attend to the oversight of their property. After the Dissolution of the Religious Orders, Conishead and its lands passed into the hands of various private owners, the Priory's Langdale possessions going to the Penningtons of Muncaster; to the family, in fact, to which the Priory owed its foundation in the 12th century.

Ecclesiastically, Clappersgate was for many centuries in the parish of Grasmere, and, until a chapel was built at Ambleside during the second half of the 15th century, to Grasmere the good folk of Clappersgate and Langdale would have to journey, in all weathers, for divine worship and for christenings, marryings and buryings. So far as these latter ministrations were concerned, it was necessary for them to go to Grasmere to be baptised, wedded and buried until 1674, for until that date the chapel at Ambleside had no parochial rights permitting it to provide these spiritual facilities.

As elsewhere in the Lake District, family names tend to recur in the Ambleside–Clappersgate area, generation after generation. Among those most frequently to be met with are those of Benson, Braithwaite, Fisher, Mackereth, Barwick, Atkinson, Airey and Forrest. Most of these were of the old "statesman" class, yeoman farmers who owned the small "estates" or holdings which they worked, and not a few of the names persist in the district today.

Not far from the confluence of the rivers Rothay and Brathay were boat landings where sailing barges could tie up to load or discharge cargoes of such commodities as wool, woven cloth, farm produce, timber and stone for building purposes. In the absence of good roads, the lake provided a convenient and relatively speedy means of transit between the remoter country areas and the markets of Ambleside, Hawkshead and Kendal, or for goods carried by sea before the port of Ravenglass silted up.

Sir John Barrow's Memorial, Ulverston

By the early part of the 17th century buildings in stone began to replace the structures of wattle and daub common in the Lake District until that time. Some of the older Clappersgate cottages undoubtedly date from this century, though some would be altered by being enlarged or given Georgian facades in the Hanoverian times. Mercifully, neither the Victorian talent for uglification nor modern trends of equal lamentability have been suffered to do much damage to the hamlet's immemorial comeliness. Only the ubiquitous motor car introduces its customary discordant notes of noise, noxious fumes and omnipresent danger. But this is a nuisance which Clappersgate has long had to learn to endure for at least the summer holiday months. Sandwiched as it is between the vast bulk of Loughrigg and the boulder-strewn Brathay, no hope of being by-passed exists to sustain it as the relentless torrent rampages past.

It is not known for certain when was built the first stone bridge over the river at this point. Almost certainly it would be a narrow structure of the packhorse variety, possibly dating from about the 14th century. At that time, and for very long after, no wider kind of crossing would be called for since no roads existed suitable for wheeled traffic until the second half of the 17th century at the earliest. It is known, however, that in 1681 the central arch of the bridge collapsed, soon after a drove of cattle had crossed over it. On this and on more than one subsequent occasion, the bridge was rebuilt and widened and the angle of approach to it modified. At its most recent renovation, in 1958, its "hump-backed" effect was reduced by the raising of the road leading to it on the Clappersgate side.

The passing of the Turnpike Act of 1761, and the erection of Toll Gates and Toll-bar cottages, led to almost immediate improvements in road surfaces, in vehicle design and in the facility of travel. And by increasing the accessibility of places like Clappersgate, these improvements led to the purchase of property by "off-comers" with money and leisure to enlarge their new acquisitions. The Croft, at Clappersgate, experienced in this way a succession of reincarnations. Originally a small farmhouse, it was bought in 1793 for £1,100 by Miss Letitia Pritchard, who transformed the place into what a contemporary writer called "a neat white seat on the shores of Lake Windermere." She spent much of the winter months elsewhere, but during the summers she entertained lavishly and occupied herself in charitable works among the poor of the hamlet. One Bella Thompson whom she befriended and took under her wing, later married Julius Caesar Ibbetson, the painter.

When Miss Pritchard died in 1827, The Croft was sold and became the property of a Liverpool sugar "king," James Brancker, who promptly pulled it down and built on the site a mansion described by Hartley Coleridge as being of a style "which neither Vitruvius, Palladio, Inigo Jones, Piranese nor Sir Jeffrey Wyattville dreamed of even in nightmare or under the influence of opium." It is only fair to say that "Li'le Hartley" also declared Brancker's new abode to be "a genial mansion where one meets with welcome, generous kindness and a great deal of strong English sense and humour, liberal politics, correct notions of ecclesiastical polity, good dinners, enough and not too much good wine, and excellent bad puns." Croft later passed into the hands of a Mrs. Fletcher, whose daughter Edith married the formidable Canon Rawnsley, founder of the National Trust. Later still, it was owned by the Cunliffe family, was eventually found to be too large for anything but the hotel it subsequently became, and having stood empty for some years, was recently (1970) advertised as being for sale. *Sic transit gloria.*

Hartley Coleridge and his brother Derwent were lodgers at Clappersgate in 1808 with a Mrs. Robinson of Rock Cottage. This good lady, it would seem, took pity upon these two little victims of a broken home, sons of an opium-crazed genius and a wronged, embittered woman, because "nobody in Ambleside would have them." One can only speculate on the particular pranks which shut the doors of the village against them, but it is good to think that they found at least a temporary refuge beneath the roof of kind Mrs. Robinson.

Adjoining Rock Cottage is Willy Hill, once the home of Julius Caesar Ibbetson and his wife, née Bella Thompson. A painting of his home done by this fine artist depicts a characteristic Westmorland farmhouse with stone mullioned windows, slate-slabbed roof, what looks uncommonly like a spinning gallery at one end, and an assortment of cows, sheep and goats companionably disposed in the adjoining lane. One of the cows is being milked on the grassy verge by what one can only describe as a distinctly buxom farm lass.

Most visitors nowadays who break their journey, so to speak, at Clappersgate probably do so in order to visit the deservedly famous garden at White Craggs—created upon a bare fell-side, in the earlier years of this century, by an orthopaedic surgeon, Mr. C. H. Hough, and devotedly tended and added to down the years by his daughters. Nowhere else in Lakeland, surely, can any private garden (as distinct from the professional nurseries) show in spring and early summer such an eye-dazzling display of rhododendrons, azaleas, flowering shrubs of infinite variety, alpines (many of very great rarity) and heathers. All are set against rocky outcrops, with winding paths leading up to a stone-flagged view-point offering a breath-taking vista down the length of Windermere. The family shrine and Calvary between a cleft in the rocks, provides the perfect climax to a work of natural beauty and harmonious co-operation between man and his Maker.

Across the bridge which spans the Brathay lies, improbably enough, the county of Lancashire in its Lakeland guise, its pastoral beauty hereabouts fully comparable with anything that either of its sister Lake Counties can boast. It requires some mental effort to link this pastoral loveliness with the dark, Satanic mills of Cotton-opolis. It is like finding a pale-faced, shawl-clad, Victorian mill girl transformed into a sturdy, apple-cheeked, laughing country wench.

And across the bridge in Lancashire is Old Brathay, consisting of a large house, a farm and farm-buildings. Once, before the house was built, a farm and an inn at this place belonged to the Braithwaite family. This was in the 17th century. The last of this name to own the property was Gawen Braithwaite, who sold it in 1788 to one George Law. This somewhat eccentric individual financially over-reached himself in converting the simple farmhouse into a mansion and in 1799, just a year after S. T. Coleridge described the house "amid these awful mountains" as "a white palace at the head of Wynandermere," the property was sold to Charles Lloyd, a member of the famous Birmingham banking family.

Lloyd took up residence at Old Brathay in 1800. Although he had begun life in the family business, the counting house suited neither his health nor his longing for the quiet ways of life. He had stayed with Coleridge at Nether Stowey in Somerset, and there had enjoyed the privilege of assisting financially that feckless genius.

It was during this period, also, that he met the Wordsworths, then living at nearby Racedown, and also Southey, whose wife Edith was sister to Coleridge's wife, Sara. Lloyd found this literary acquaintance congenial, and no doubt the return of the Wordsworths to the Lake Country, to be followed soon after by the arrival of the Coleridges and Southeys at Greta Hall, Keswick, decided the former Quaker banker in his choice of residence after his marriage.

At Old Brathay, Lloyd and his charming young wife spent several happy years, entertaining widely and making the house a centre of literary society and activity. In addition to the three "lions" already mentioned and their families, the "white palace" which Lloyd had bought from George Law sheltered at various times others of that gifted band who shed their lustre on the Lake Country in the early years of the 19th century. Here might be seen (and heard) Professor John Wilson of Elleray ("Christopher North"), Thomas De Quincey, Mrs. Hemans, Bishop Watson of Calgarth (and occasionally Llandaff, of which he was nominally the chief pastor), Miss Fenwick, and many another of lesser fame.

Delighting in the company of such kindred souls and rejoicing in the affection of their young family, the Lloyds passed at Old Brathay the happiest years they were to have together. Later, as the children grew to maturity, a nervous disability took increasing hold of the once company-loving Lloyd and he shrank more and more from outside contacts. The house, which had hitherto echoed the animated talk of men and women of letters mingled with the happy laughter of children, now relapsed into a tragic and unaccustomed gloom. In the year of Waterloo Lloyd left Old Brathay for medical treatment in Birmingham and never returned. His malady grew worse. In 1818 he entered a mental home in York. After a temporary recovery, he lived in London for a few years and then settled in France in 1823. Here the trouble returned, and poor Charles Lloyd, who had known such complete contentment beside the clear waters of the Brathay, died in a French nursing home in 1839, far from the Lakeland of his unclouded years.

Lloyd's son Owen took Holy Orders and became parish priest of Langdale. He was a gentle, happy soul, greatly beloved by all who knew him. Alas, the same malign disease which was to darken his father's later years struck this blithe and generous creature and he died, all too young, in 1831. He is still remembered as the author of the Rushbearing Hymn, composed at Ambleside when he was assistant curate to old Parson Dawes and a lodger at the Post Office, now a coach company's office.

Brathay Hall, or High Brathay, was the home of the Harden family at about the same period of the Lloyds' residence next door. The Hardens, in 1804, moved to Brathay from Edinburgh where John Harden, an amateur artist of considerable ability, had married another painter, Jessie Allan, who was a pupil of James Nasmyth and daughter of a prominent Scottish banker. Harden found abundant subjects for his sketch book in his new surroundings. He also found highly congenial the literary society into which the Lloyds soon introduced him. But now the poets and essayists were reinforced by a number of painters who found a lesser or greater degree of inspiration in the Lakeland scene. Among those entertained by the Hardens at Brathay Hall were John Constable, Henry Raeburn and Joseph Farington. Even the purely literary circle was expanding. Now were to be met with by Brathayside the Arnolds from Fox How, the statesman George Canning, Crabbe Robinson, Mrs. Gaskell and many less eminent practitioners of the pen.

In 1834 the Hardens left Brathay Hall for Field Head, Hawkshead. John Harden's son Joseph, like Owen Lloyd, took Holy Orders and, like Owen again, found congenial spheres of work among the lakes and mountains, first as assistant curate at Hawkshead and later as Vicar of Coniston.

The Hardens were followed at Brathay by the Redmaynes who proved generous benefactors to the area, Mr. Giles Redmayne providing the cost of building a new church in 1836. The increased population, and the ever-present problem of journeying to Ambleside for worship over bad roads in wintry weather, had long indicated that a church at Brathay was required. The site chosen was a fine one. It consisted of a hilly piece of land, given by the Cookson family, looking down on the tumbling waters of the Brathay far below. The flat ground on the summit measured less than 30,000 square yards, and this circumstance enforced the "orientation" of the new building to be North by South, instead of the usual East by West. Wordsworth praised the site highly, remarking that it compared very favourably with the situation of many an alpine mountain church. Whether the poet approved equally of the church's architectural style is more open to doubt. It was built in an Italianate manner, showing little in common with the rugged, four-square simplicity of the mountain chapels of the Lake Counties or with Cumbrian building styles in general.

As soon as the church was completed, a parish was formed out of the ancient parishes of Hawkshead and Grasmere. Later a Vicarage, a Day School and a Sunday School were added, and for more than a century Brathay had a flourishing and independent parochial life of its own. Recently, however, the changed conditions of modern life have forced a reversion to older patterns of administration. No longer a separate parish, Brathay is now served from Ambleside and its Vicarage provides the official residence of the Suffragan Bishop of Penrith.

In between the two World Wars, the Redmayne family sold Brathay Hall to Mr. F. C. Scott of Matson Ground, who most generously provisionally vested it in the National Trust. During the last War it gave shelter to children of Nursery School age from London and the East Coast. With the ending of hostilities the question of the property's future came again to the forefront, and it was decided to combine the Old Brathay and Brathay Hall estates in order to provide a centre of outdoor activites on "Outward Bound" lines. Residential courses are run all the year round for boys and girls from schools in urban areas and from industry. In addition to open-air pursuits such as climbing, walking, sailing, canoeing, camping, etc., there are indoor courses of a cultural kind embracing drama, art, sculpture and sundry crafts. One likes to think of the shades of former occupants of the two mansions—Lloyds, Hardens, Redmaynes, Bells, Lubbocks—surveying all that goes on around Brathay today with surprise, maybe, but also with understanding and goodwill.

WORDSWORTH IN EASEDALE

IN the autumn of the year 1839 Lancrigg, a small farm under Helm Crag, in the valley of Easedale, near Grasmere, became vacant and for sale. It was purchased almost at once by a Mrs. Elizabeth Fletcher, the widow of a prominent Edinburgh advocate and Whig Reformer. Mrs. Fletcher and her family had frequently stayed for holidays in the neighbourhood of Grasmere, several times at Thorney How which adjoined the Lancrigg property.

Mrs. Fletcher was a lady of great beauty and intellect. In Edinburgh she had moved freely in leading literary and political circles, numbering among her friends such celebrated figures as Allan Cunningham, Lord Brougham, Joanna Baillie, Sir Walter Scott, Lord Cockburn and the Italian patriot Mazzini. In the Lakes she had at once been accepted on terms of intimate friendship by the famous Dr. Arnold and his family at Fox How, by the Hardens of Brathay Hall, by the Southeys at Greta Hall, Keswick, and, most gratifyingly of all perhaps, by the great poet and his family at Rydal Mount. It was, in fact, no less a person than Wordsworth himself who acted on Mrs. Fletcher's behalf in the negotiations over the purchase of Lancrigg.

Mrs. Fletcher had two sons, Miles and Angus, and four daughters, Elizabeth, Grace, Margaret and Mary. The third of these daughters had married, in March 1830, Dr. John Davy, brother of the famous Sir Humphry. Mary was later, in August 1847, to marry Sir John Richardson, naturalist and Arctic explorer.*

Both younger daughters kept diaries, and after Wordsworth's death in 1850 Mrs. Davy expanded her memories of the poet for the benefit of her children. So far as is known, these reminiscences have never been published, though Mrs. Moorman makes a brief reference to (and quotation from) them in her great biography of Wordsworth.

---

*For a fuller account of the Fletchers of Lancrigg the reader is referred to *Lake Country Portraits*: H. A. L. Rice (Harvill Press, 1967), Chapter 7.

Mrs. Davy thus records on:

January 16th, 1844: "An agreeable little dinner party (at Lancrigg)—Mr. Wordsworth, Miss Fenwick, Mr. Crabbe Robinson and others. Mr. Wordsworth, on entering our parlour, seemed to have about him the remains of some unpleasant mood of mind, but very soon after sitting down to dinner the cloud cleared from his venerable face and, as it seemed, from his mind. My mother and he went back to reminiscences of the olden time—the early days of the French Revolution. He spoke of Helen Maria Williams, and of Mrs. Charlotte Smith, on which my mother took up an old favourite sonnet of hers:

'Queen of the silver bow—by the pale beam . . .'
and she and Mr. Wordsworth repeated it together in a sort of duet, their fine voices in happy contrast.

"On coming into the little parlour after dinner, he began to speak of the annoyances to which authors—and poets especially —are subject from criticism, and then more particularly of the various criticisms to which his lately composed epitaph* had been exposed. We thought that he met very eloquently one of the objections made by his nephew, Dr. Christopher Wordsworth, Headmaster of Harrow, to the concluding lines of the epitaph:

'But he to Heaven was vowed
Thro' a life long and pure,
And Christian faith calmed in his soul
the fear of change and death.'

"Dr. Wordsworth had observed in a letter to the Poet that day: 'You might have said the same of any ordinary Christian.' 'Now,' said Mr. Wordsworth, 'I know of nothing ordinary or extraordinary in relation to a man as a Christian. If he is really a Christian and conforms in practice to his faith, then, be he what he may, he is the highest type of man. Highly as I thought of Southey, it never occurred to me that as a Christian he could differ from any other, or be more exalted than any other'."

---

*On Robert Southey, for his memorial in Crosthwaite Church, Keswick. Southey had died on 25th July 1843, and Wordsworth had been appointed to succeed him as Poet Laureate.

January 22nd: "While Mrs. Quillinan* was sitting with us, H. Fletcher† ran in to say that he must be off to Oxford within the hour . . . Some of us went down with him to the Mail. We met Mr. W. at the Post Office in charming mood—his spirits excited by the sunshine. We entered at once on a full flow of discourse, introduced I cannot say how, and continued as we walked to and fro, waiting the arrival of the Mail, first on the evil of allowing knowledge of natural things to take the place either of enjoyment in those, or of devotion to the Author and Giver. He mentioned the common saying, from Chaucer downwards, of a physician's being naturally undevout. He looked benevolently on H.F. as he mounted the coach, and seemed quite disposed to give an old man's blessing to the young man setting forth on an untried field, and then, no wise interrupted by the hurrying to and fro of ostlers with their steaming horses, or passengers with their carpet bags, he launched into a dissertation in which there was, I thought, a remarkable union of his powerful diction and his practical good sense—on the subject of College habits, and of his utter distrust of all attempts to nurse virtue by an avoidance of temptation."

"On the 6th of March Mr. W. went with us to—, and during the drive mentioned with marked pleasure a dedication written by Mr, Keble‡ and sent to him for his approval and permission to have it prefixed to Mr. Keble's new volume of Latin Lectures on Poetry given at Oxford. Mr. W. said that he had never seen any estimate of his poetic powers, or more especially of his aim in poetry that seemed to him so discriminating and so satisfactory."

Another famous name appears in Mrs. Davy's reminiscences later that year. On July 16th she writes:

"Mr. and Mrs. W. dined with us. He spoke of Charles James Fox and mentioned (the only such mention I ever heard from him) 'a *bon mot* of my own'. It was when Fox and he were

---

*Wordsworth's greatly-loved daughter, Dora.

†Henry Fletcher, son of Mrs. Davy's brother, Miles. Henry later took Holy Orders and ultimately became Rector of Grasmere from 1878 to 1893.

‡The Reverend John Keble of Oriel, Professor of Poetry at Oxford, and one of the founding fathers of the Tractarian Movement.

introduced to each other in London at one of the great Whig houses.* Fox rose from a table (a card table, I think) at which he was seated and as he advanced to meet the poet he said 'I am glad to see Mr. Wordsworth, though we differ as much in our views of Politics as we do in our views of Poetry.' 'To which', said Wordsworth, 'I replied: "You must admit that in Poetry I am the Whig and you the Tory".' This meeting took place in 1806, only a few weeks before Fox's death."

It was on this occasion at Lancrigg that Wordsworth, so Mrs. Davy remembered, spoke of his old friend and collaborator, S. T. Coleridge.

"Mr. and Mrs. Price (Mr. Bonamy Price, afterwards Professor of Political Economy at Oxford), with two lady relatives and Mr. Rose, a brother of Mrs. Price's and a devout admirer of Wordsworth, joined us later. A circle was made as large as our little parlour could hold. Mr. Price sat next to Mr. W., and by design or fortunate accident introduced some remark on the powers and discourse of Coleridge. Mr. W. entered heartily on this subject. He said that the liveliest and truest image he could give of Coleridge's talk was that of a majestic river, the sound or sight of its course being those which one caught at intervals—sometimes concealed by forests, sometimes lost in sand, then flashing out broad and distinct, then again taking a turn which one's eye could not follow though one knew it to be the same river . . . Mr. W. went on to say that in his opinion Coleridge had been spoiled as a poet by going to Germany; that the bent of his mind, which was at all times very much towards metaphysical theology, had there been fixed in that direction.

"From Coleridge the talk then turned to Scott, and Mr. W., in his best manner and with earnestness and in noble diction, gave his reasons for thinking that as a poet Scott would not live. 'I don't like,' he said, 'to say all this or to take to pieces some of his best reputed passages, especially in the presence of my wife because she thinks me too fastidious,† but as a poet he cannot live for he has never, in verse, written anything

---

*Holland House?

†An interesting sidelight, this, on the normally unobtrusive Mary Wordsworth!

addressed to the immortal part of man.' As a prose author, Mr.
W. admitted that Scott had touched a higher vein, because
there he had really dealt with feelings and passions. As historical
novels, professing to give the manners and customs of the past,
he (Mr. W.) did not attach much value to the works of Scott,
holding them to be an attempt to succeed where success was
impossible."

Whatever may be thought of this last generalisation, which
Wordsworth might well have modified had he lived to read the
works of some modern writers of historical fiction, it will probably
be widely agreed that the most recent dispassionate estimate of
Scott's literary genius does not differ greatly from that of his friend
and contemporary, Wordsworth.

On matters religious, Mrs. Davy was "glad to note," in her
recorded remembrances at the beginning of 1845:

". . . some really interesting discourse from W. At the
beginning of the evening he was grave and silent. On something
being said, however, relating to the present state of the Church,
he opened his own views and gave expression, as I have only
once heard him do before, to his own humble, devout faith.
Speaking of St. Paul, 'Oh, what a character that is!' he said.
'How well we know him; how human, yet how noble; how
little his outward sufferings moved him. It is not in thinking of
them that he calls himself wretched, but when speaking of the
inward conflict.'

" 'Paul and David,' he went on, 'may be called the two
Shakespearian characters of the Bible; both types, as it were, of
human nature in its strength and weakness. Moses is grand, but
then it is chiefly from position, from the office entrusted to
him. We do not know him as a brother man'."

Early in 1846, while her husband was abroad on medical duties
of a more or less official nature, Mrs. Davy records a visit she paid
to Rydal Mount:

"Went today to pay my respects to the Poet on his birthday,
April 7th. He seemed pleased. Both he and dear Mrs. W. very
happy in the arrival of their four grandsons; the three elder to
go to school at Rossall next week. Some talk concerning schools

led Mr. W. into a discourse, which I thought very interesting, on the dangers of emulation. He had written very lately to his nephew Charles remarking on a sermon of his, preached as a farewell to his Winchester pupils, speaking of emulation as a help to school progress. Mr. W. thinks that envy is likely to go along with this, and therefore would hold it to be unsafe. 'In my own case,' he said, 'I never felt emulation with another man but once, and that was accompanied by envy—it's a horrid feeling! This was in the study of Italian, which I entered on at College along with ——. I never engaged in the proper studies of the University, so that I had no temptation in those to envy anyone. But I remember with pain that I had envious feelings when my fellow-student in Italian got before me. I was his superior in many mental departments, but he was the better Italian scholar and I envied him. The annoyance this gave me made me feel that emulation was not for me, and it made me very thankful that as a boy I had never experienced it.' In the course of the conversation Mr. W. said, smiling: 'One other time in my life I felt envy. It was when my brother was nearly certain of success in a foot race with me. I tripped up his heels; this must have been envy.' 'It was worse,' quoth Mrs. W. 'It was malice. Oh, William! very bad indeed.' Mr. —— came in before I left the Mount today, and enjoyed as I did the pleasant flow of talk in the Poet of 76."

January 11th, 1847: "Met Mr. W. He turned with me to L. How* and something led to the mention of Milton whose poetry, he said, was early more a favourite with him than that of Shakespeare. Speaking of Milton's not allowing his daughters to learn Greek, or at least not exerting himself to teach it to them, he admitted that this seemed to betoken a low impression of the condition and purposes of a woman's mind. 'And yet,' Mr. W. went on, 'where could he have picked up such notions in a country which had seen so many women of learning and ability? But his opinion of what women ought to be, it may be presumed, is given in his Eve as contrasted with the right condition of man,

He for God only, she for God in him.
Now that is a low, a very low, and a very false estimate of

---

*Lesketh How, the Ambleside home of Dr. and Mrs. Davy.

woman's condition.' Mr. W. was amused at my showing him
the almost contemporary notice of Milton by Wycherley, and
after reading it spoke a good deal of the obscurity of men of genius
in or near their own time. He had just been reading, he said,
Miss Strickland's Life of Queen Elizabeth* in which hardly (*sic*)
or nothing of Shakespeare was to be found. 'But,' he continued,
'the most singular thing is that in all the works of Bacon there
is not an allusion to Shakespeare'."

Later in the same spring Mrs. Davy has to record the great
sorrow of the ageing poet in the mortal illness of his beloved
daughter Dora.

> *April* 29*th* 1847: "My notebook says—A mournful visit from
> Mr. W. . . . yet it is a comfort now, and will always be a pleasure
> to remember that his gentleness in the hour of grief, his uncom-
> plainingness as to any person or circumstance connected with
> the sad event, were exactly such as Christianity, and that only,
> teaches to an affectionate and afflicted heart."

Dora (Mrs. Quillinan) died on July 9th. A few days later, Mrs.
Davy remembered her impression of the bereaved father's self-
composure.

> "Those who saw her father after her death were surprised by
> his calmness. The close of the weary suffering was a relief to
> him and to her dear, admirable mother, but there were sad
> days to them both to come afterwards. The 14th of July was
> the funeral day. No friends were invited, but Mrs. Arnold†
> and I went to Grasmere Church to pray along with those deep
> mourners . . . I shall long remember the still, soft, warm summer
> beauty of that morning. Never were life, the joyous summer
> life of Nature, and Death and bereavement more solemnly and
> sadly contrasted than on that day."

The following year, 1848, Mrs. Davy records a visit from Mr.
Wordsworth on a summer evening, on the occasion of the Ambleside
Rushbearing:

> "After seeing the field party out of doors, we had a large
> miscellaneous one within. The presence of Judge Crampton
> emboldened me to ask Mr. W. to join us and when we were all

---

*In *Lives of the Queens of England* by Agnes Strickland, 1840–48.
†Widow of Dr. Thomas Arnold of Rugby, and then still living at Fox How, Rydal.

assembled he came in. When he and the 'upright Judge' sat down in the middle of the room to converse we were all delighted with the beauty of their heads. They were, indeed, unusually fine in form. Mr. W. seemed to take pleasure in the interview, and when the party dispersed some of us escorted Mr. W. to the foot of his Mount. I am sure, dear A., you will not forget the still beauty of that evening. Nothing interrupted it but the note of a bird which I did not know till Mr. W. said it was one of the notes of the owl . . . and in this he was confirmed by his servant James, who had come to meet his master with a cloak to keep the night air from hurting him.''

Monday, April 22nd, 1850: "I had some talk which interested me much today with good Mrs. Nicholson at the (Ambleside) Post Office, concerning Mr. W. She has known him perhaps longer than anyone here, and in her simple, homely, hearty manner does as full justice to his sweet and fine qualities as anyone could do. She went back, in the manner of the old, on her earlier days of acquaintance with the poet and his sister—when they lived at Grasmere—and when, as she said, they (i.e., William and Dorothy) would often walk to Ambleside together after dark in order to repair some omission or alter some arrangement in the proof sheets of his poems, which had been posted for the press. 'At that time,' said Mrs. Nicholson, 'the Mail used to pass through at one in the morning, so my husband and me used to go early to bed, but when Mr. and Miss Wordsworth came, let it be as late as it would, my husband would get up and let them in, and give them their letter out of the box, and then they would sit in our parlour or in the kitchen discussing over it, and reading and changing, till they had made it quite to their minds. Then they would seal up the packet again, and knock at our bedroom door, and say, 'Now, Mrs. Nicholson, please will you bolt the door after us? Here is our letter for the post. We'll not trouble you any more this night.' And, oh, they were always so friendly to us, and so loving to one another'."

Tuesday, April 23rd: "On returning from his early visit to (Rydal) Mount this morning, your father (i.e. Dr. Davy) told me that Mr. W. was dying but still conscious, knowing those about him. It must have been about half-past ten when your father left him. It seems that soon after eleven the difficulty of breathing increased, and the sound in the throat indicating that the end was very near, all in the house were summoned to his bedside. He said something, not very articulate, but supposing it to refer to the Commendatory Prayer for the Departing his son John read that passage of the last service, and his father showed some satisfaction in having been understood. Exactly at 12, when, as old Mrs. Cookson told me, 'the cuckoo clock was singing noon,' he passed gently away.

"As soon as the last breath was drawn, Mrs. W. went to his poor sister and said to her 'He is gone to Dora.' The poor old lady (Dorothy Wordsworth) received the tidings with unusual calmness; indeed during the whole illness she has been gently patient.

"This departure is a heart sorrow. There is no saying how much of the interest of life it takes from the valley in our daily walk. And then we have to think of the sorrowing loneliness of her who loved him better than her life, and who knew herself to be beloved as few can deserve to be in like degree. The simplest prose could not better express all that Mrs. W. actually is, than do those sonnets of finished poetical beauty which he has addressed to her picture. There can indeed be little earthly brightness for her affectionate spirit now, but I can believe that this night she is earnestly thanking God for his release from pain and weariness, and from the grief of being the survivor as she is now."

On April 25th Dr. and Mrs. Davy went to Rydal Mount, at Mrs. Wordsworth's invitation, to take their last sight of the dead poet. After commenting at some length upon the gentleness and repose of the expression upon his face, Mrs. Davy remembered how her husband had been struck by a remarkable likeness to portraits he had seen of Dante. Mrs. Davy, too, was struck by this resemblance.

" . . . I thought if the laurel wreath had been there, it would have been nearly the same face as that which we see in the portraits considered authentic of that poet of an older time.

"There is an article in yesterday's *The Times*, well-written, wisely and kindly, but, oh, it seems so cold to what we are all feeling in the extinction of this light of our valley, this household, neighbourly remembrancer of high and pure thoughts. But let us be thankful for the privilege of having had some intercourse with him. Let us cherish the thoughts of his simplicity, his love of Nature, his Benevolence for his brother man in all conditions. He had cast aside all speculative democracy, but he was practically democratic in no common degree. In the frugality of his habits, the considerate attention to his servants, the sociable conversing intercourse which he kept up with persons inferior in the scale of society according to ordinary estimates, he was admirable as an example in the small community in which he lived. In all such respects, his life was a constant illustration of his verse, a living protest against all that was artificial or false, or ungentle in the conventional notions and arrangements of our modern life."

NOTE: These extracts from Mrs. Davy's diary were found, after his death, among the papers of my step-father, the late Anthony A. Fletcher, great-great-nephew of Mrs. Davy. They appear to have been copied by my step-father at some early period of his life. As he never mentioned them to me, I presume he had forgotten their existence!   H.A.L.R.

The Vale of Grasmere, Easedale

Herdwick sheep in Langdale

BEASTS AND FEATHERED FOWLS

I THINK St. Francis would have loved the English Lake Country. Quite apart from the scenery, the birds and beasts hereabouts have an engaging quality and a friendliness all their own. No doubt the desire for food has a great deal to do with it, but one can forgive the Watendlath chaffinches their greed as they hop about pecking at the crumbs on one's very lunch table. And a similar tolerance must be extended to the Herdwick sheep, at the summit of Honister, who unashamedly make up to the passing pedestrian in no doubt well-founded expectation of some succulent trifle.

The small flock of barnacle geese, whose lunch I disturbed near Friar's Crag on Derwentwater one May morning, were probably themselves only making a short stay in Cumberland, before journeying on to more northerly climes. Yet they seemed to have captured some of the glad, confident friendliness of the local resident bird-life, and exhibited neither fear nor annoyance at my intrusion.

A day or two later I sat on a seat near Borran's Field at Ambleside, watching the white wings of yachts as they tacked gracefully if a trifle inconsequently upon the sparkling waters of Windermere. As I sat clutching my right ankle, a Westmorland robin perched itself upon my shoe within a couple of inches of my hand. Robins everywhere are notorious for their boldness but something, I felt, of the old Viking spirit must have been bred in this particular specimen of his race.

That same day, walking back towards Rydal, I derived considerable pleasure from watching the transference of a flock of Herdwicks, with their lambs, from a field on the Loughrigg side of the main road to Rydal Park on the other. Because of the lambs, the somewhat disorderly procession moved rather slowly. Every so often a particularly exuberant and unco-operative lamb would try to make a bolt for it, back to the pasture which was being vacated. At once he would be pursued by an outraged Border Collie sheep-dog and, if

St. Andrew's church, Greystoke
Sizergh Castle

he continued recalcitrant, would be firmly but gently bowled over—just to remind him that discipline must be maintained.

It was amusing to see that the ewes were foremost in crossing the road; the lambs, bunched together at the rear, apparently playing a gregarious version of "last across." Once inside the Park, the ewes immediately began to sample the pasture new with evident satisfaction. After a few mouthfuls, however, their sense of maternal responsibility suddenly reasserted itself. A positive concerto of bleating broke out, as each anxious mother dashed madly and confusedly about in search of her own precious offspring. The confusion proved to be of brief duration, the various families were quickly reunited, and afternoon tea was taken by all concerned.

*   *   *   *

It was a glorious spring evening when I decided to re-visit the Stone Circle on Castlerigg, near Keswick. This was not to be, however, the usual solitary contemplation I had hitherto enjoyed at this ancient haunt of pre-historic man. I found myself forestalled by a bevy, not mercifully of gaping tourists, but of enthusiastic young bullocks. Recently turned out from the stock-yard to judge by the condition of their coats, they were full of the joys of spring and eagerly inspecting the massive limestone monoliths. Upon my appearance they joyfully abandoned archaeology and crowded round me with all the unabashed curiosity of Muscovite citizens examining an American automobile.

Their attentions, I felt, were flattering but a trifle ill-timed. I had come to ponder less tangible and contemporary matters, and I turned away with what I hoped was an air of dignified if not un-friendly finality. I moved austerely away, circumnavigating the stones. The bullocks decided to come along too. They fell in happily behind, even jostling one another for the privilege of walking behind me. When I paused to examine one of the monoliths, one or two of the bolder spirits would sidle up closer and nuzzle me with warm but over-moist affection.

I had no wish to seem ungrateful for their obvious admiration, but I began to feel that enough was enough. I had visions of myself marching into Keswick at the head of a column of adoring young beeves; so, taking advantage of a momentary diversion caused by the passing of a car in the lonning nearby and abandoning pre-history and my bovine fans, I passed silently and rapidly from the scene.

Back on the road I waved cheerfully, as one who has rid himself of an embarrassing incubus, to a farmer rounding up sheep in a field, The farmer waved affably back, just as I passed the open gate through which the sheep were to be driven. Seconds later I became aware of a steady pitter-patter of hooves behind me. One backward glance was enough to inform me that I was indeed heading a column towards Keswick—not of bullocks but of Herdwick ewes and their young.

We proceeded (as the police reports invariably put it) in a Keswick-wards direction, thus: myself (somewhat self-consciously, I confess); some fifty or sixty ewes with a full complement of lambs; a blasé looking sheepdog; two small boys with sticks; the farmer—now at the wheel of a small van. Where we all might have ended up there is no saying, but, suddenly, from around the next turn in the lane appeared four young girls. One was riding a grey pony, the other three were walking. One of these latter was leading a lamb on a dog's chain and collar. These reinforcements fell in beside me at the head of the parade and we pressed on, chatting lightly of this and that.

The young ladies, it seemed, were either daughters or nieces of the van-driving farmer away back at the end of the retinue. They had come to escort the convoy to its home base. This proved to be Field Place Farm, at the entrance to which my young companions took up stations across the road and headed the sheep into the farmyard, for the purpose of some unspecified but no doubt beneficial operation. Farewells exchanged, and relieved of my command, I journeyed on alone.

Well, almost alone. Crossing the river Greta by Calvert Bridge, I came to Windebrowe. Here I was at once joined by a cheerful and unattached Lakeland terrier, whose "I'm-so-glad-you-have-turned-up" expression reminded me of those Druidical young bullocks. Together, in silent communion, we covered the next quarter of a mile or so until my latest companion, suddenly remembering perhaps that he had to see a dog about a man, disappeared abruptly in the direction of Spooney Green Farm.

It was with almost a feeling of resentment that I noted that the hotel cat, with whom I had a passing acquaintance, was nowhere to be seen as I arrived at journey's end.

*   *   *   *

For the lover of wild life who goes about with his eyes open, Lakeland is full of sudden and unlooked-for delights. Recently I stopped my car to watch a kestrel hovering for minutes almost directly overhead, poised motionless with even its wing movements in abeyance. Suddenly it dropped like a bomb on some hidden prey in the road-side verge, only to rise sharply almost at once, empty-handed so to speak. One could imagine him snarling "Foiled again!" like the frustrated villain of some Victorian melodrama. However, he flew off philosophically enough, no doubt to resume his routine of hover and swoop elsewhere.

It was an unusually warm afternoon for late March, and as I turned into the main Keswick–Penrith road I was amused to see the impressive figure of a short-eared owl "a-taking of his *dolce far niente*" on the stone wall flanking the road. Blissfully unheeding the passing traffic, he dozed contentedly in the unaccustomed sunshine.

On the high moorland to the south of this busy road, a small flock of these large and not so common birds had been in residence throughout the winter, and several times I had stopped to watch them quartering the ground with powerful swoops of their three-foot-span wings, searching amongst the heather for the small creatures which constitute their diet. From time to time I would see one alight on a Forestry Commission fencing post. Here he would contemplate the upland scene, turning his almost spherical head in that disconcerting way that owls have, through a circuit of apparently three hundred and sixty degrees.

The kestrel, poised on motionless wings, is a familiar enough sight hereabouts, and so is the buzzard soaring with splendid arrogance around the fell tops. But it must have been the hard weather we had in February which brought one foraging at ground level, one wintry day in the Mungrisdale area. His presence was clearly resented by the resident crows, however, and some of them proceeded to "mob" him—until he flew languidly away towards Souther Fell with the lofty disdain of an aristocrat jostled by *sans culottes*.

Motoring along the Lakeland side roads in spring time requires extra caution; rounding a bend rather too sharply, you may find yourself swerving to avoid one or more wandering and unattended sheep. Many flocks are brought down from the remoter fells at this season for lambing and, finding little in the way of grass to nibble, they take to wandering about in search of pastures new. The attractive Herdwick is especially given to this and, with her goat-like agility in leaping, stone walls avail to restrain neither her exits nor her entrances once she has made up her mind to wander. And having found a supply of fresh, uncropped grass, she will return to it again and again. Like the elephant, she never forgets. I had new grass laid down in my garden in the autumn, and early in the New Year this fresh young growth was joyfully discovered by three foot-loose Herdwicks from a flock based on a farm more than a mile away. Driven out with sticks, stones and maledictions, and moved smartly on by my neighbour's sheepdogs, still they came back. In the end transportation by Land-Rover (their owner's) to some far-distant fell-side relieved me of their embarrassing attendance.

Hares, too, take to frequenting the highway at this season of the year. Caught in a car's headlights, they tend to flee down the middle of the road instead of taking to the verges and the hedgerows. In their panic they are liable to tack unpredictably from side to side, and it is not always easy to avoid running over them. Many a spring morning a pathetic bundle of fur by the roadside tells of the untimely end of a hare whose March madness led him to forsake the safety of the fields for the fatal roadway. Later in the year it will be the mangled remains of hedgehogs which will all too often tell the same sad tale.

This, of course, is fox-hunting country, and it was no uncommon sight for me to see hounds in full cry streaming across the broad face of the fell facing my cottage. One day a few winters ago, when all was white with snow, a fox leapt the wall into the field just below my garden. Padding across the firm white surface in a surprisingly unhurried way, he leapt the next wall with equal ease and so passed from my range of vision. Two or three minutes later, and with contrasting noise and urgency, came the chiming hounds in full pursuit.

On Mid-Lent Sunday, I spotted a large red dog fox trotting calmly across another neighbour's field which flanked the road. He, too, showed no sign of furtiveness or hurry. Perhaps he knew what day of the week it was—a *dies non* so far as hunting is concerned.

A particularly engaging occasional visitor who came to my Matterdale garden invariably did seem pressed for time. He was a bright-eyed little stoat—not everyone's pet, perhaps, but utterly fascinating to watch, with his quick-silver dartings among the shrubs, his sudden lightning leaps up the dry-stone wall and down again, and his equally sudden halts to sit up on his hind legs to survey the scene. Usually I saw him in his smart beige summer suiting, with only his soft white waistcoat to remind one of his winter ermine. But on the last day of March I saw him hurrying anxiously across the rose bed, with what appeared to be a mouse dangling from his mouth. His coat looked to be in a transitional stage, the white of winter giving way to a more seasonable shade of fawn. A few days later, however, the vale was blanketed in snow, and I could not help wondering whether he had perforce changed back again into winter camouflage.

With April the curlew can be expected, filling the dale once more with his sad complaining. Soon, too, the wheatears will be back, flashing their white rumps in every hedge-row, to be followed at no great distance of time by the redstarts and yellow-hammers in colourful competition. By May the cuckoo will have arrived, with his slow purposeful flight and his monotonous advertising of his presence from the spinney in the dale bottom. The spotted fly-catchers, the wagtails (pied and yellow), the swallows, swifts and martins will all be welcome additions to our company of faithful winter residents—robin, chaffinch, tits, dunnock, wren, blackbird, thrush and the handsome pair of bullfinches whom I, not having any fruit trees, would like to welcome to the garden more often. But, like their cousins, the greenfinch and the goldfinch, one sees them all too infrequently.

Perhaps when summer comes I shall achieve a long-standing ambition and see, at dusk, a live badger on the prowl. There are plenty about in these parts, but they are shy nocturnal creatures and, not myself being a night bird, I have so far seen only a dead one by the road-side. But one never knows. The rich and varied wild-life of Lakeland is full of agreeable surprises. Recently in the Vale of Newlands I had a ring-side view of a red squirrel foraging for hazel nuts. I had feared the species was extinct in the Lake Counties.

But of all four-footed creatures, none to my mind is more typical of the Lake Country, none more friendly and attractive, certainly none more useful to man (now that the horse, alas, has been banished from our farms) than the ubiquitous and hard-working Border Collie sheep-dog. Anyone who attends the Sheep Dog Trials held at Troutbeck, Rydal, Threlkeld, Patterdale and elsewhere during the summer months cannot fail to be impressed by the astonishing intelligence of these animals. Guided only by a series of whistles from its owner or handler, each competitor will manoeuvre three or four wayward and unpredictable sheep over a marked-out course, between a succession of gate-posts, and will finally pen them into a small space formed by hurdles. The successful dog, of course, is the one which performs this task in the shortest time.

On the farm and on the fell, the Border sheep-dog's sagacity is matched by his appetite for work, his endurance, fleetness of foot and apparent indifference to weather conditions. His thick, glossy coat of black and white renders him impervious to wind and rain, and in snow he positively appears to revel. As for speed, he seems to run uphill almost as fleetly as on the flat.

It is, of course, for their quite uncanny intelligence, their infallible interpretation of their handlers' wishes and their instant obedience that these dogs are most remarkable. These characteristics are partly the result of breeding; even quite young, untrained puppies may be seen instinctively rounding up indignant hens and penning them firmly in a corner of the farmyard.

But training plays a vital role in the making of a good working sheep-dog, and great patience is called for on the part of his trainer. The young dog learns something from the example of his canine seniors, but it is from his trainer that he must learn the finer points of his job. He must learn to interpret the different meanings of a variety of shrill whistles, all of which may sound much alike to the uninitiated but to the dog can mean either "Go left," "Go right," "Stand still," "Lie down" or "Come to heel." He must learn patience, obedience, perseverance and to restrain his natural exuberance. It is small wonder that generations of such training have produced a breed of unsurpassed intelligence and eagerness to work. The Border Collie—alert, handsome, affectionate—inherits a disposition which makes him the fell farmer's most valued colleague and friend.

GREYSTOKE CHURCH

THE village of Greystoke (anciently Graystock) lies on the line of the old Roman road from Voreda (Old Penrith) to Keswick and Derventio (Papcastle), near Cockermouth, and from earliest times there must have been always a fair amount of traffic (on foot and horseback until the 18th century) passing through. It seems likely that the 6th century missionary, St. Kentigern, whose name is preserved in the dedication of churches at Keswick (Crosthwaite), Mungrisdale and Castle Sowerby, made use of this ancient highway and so most probably would St. Cuthbert, a century or so later, when he came from Northumberland to visit his friend St. Herbert at his island hermitage on Derwentwater.

Unlike so many of the Lakeland churches, St. Andrew's, Greystoke is of noble proportions outwardly and refreshingly spacious within. This is due to the fact that in the 14th century it became a collegiate church, with a master and six chaplains. It is not known when the earliest church on this site was built, but Thomas de Vipont,* Rector of Greystoke, became Bishop of Carlisle in 1255—the earliest ecclesiastical mention of the parish.

Nor is it known when the Church was consecrated, nor why St. Andrew should have been chosen for patron saint. It has been suggested, however, that since Greystoke (along with Penrith and Dacre, whose churches are similarly dedicated) was from the 7th century to the 9th in the diocese of Hexham, and since the fine Abbey Church at Hexham was also dedicated to St. Andrew (in 674 A.D.), this fact may have some bearing upon the choice.

In 1291 the living of Greystoke was entered in the *Valor* of Pope Nicholas at £120 a year—the richest benefice in Cumberland at that time. The bishopric of Carlisle was then only worth £126 7s. p.a. But by 1318 the value of the living of Greystoke had fallen to only £20, and, through the non-residence of its rector, Ralph de Ergholme (1314 to 1357), and through general neglect, the chancel and parsonage house were in a state of dilapidation. Better days

*Or Veteripont.

came, however, in the middle of the century. A new rector, Richard de Hoton Roof, took out a commission of inquiry into the state of the buildings in 1357, as a consequence of which William, fourteenth Lord of Greystoke* gave the church its collegiate foundation. An alabaster effigy of a knight, now at the west end of the south aisle, is believed to represent this same Lord of Greystoke.

Later in the 14th century, when the Bishop of Carlisle ordered a visitation to be held, it was disclosed that the church was still in a considerable state of disrepair, its walls ruinous, the belfry collapsed and the roof largely open to the sky. Repairs were at once ordered and the parishioners threatened with excommunication unless they contributed promptly to the same.

It was at this time that Ralph, Lord of Greystoke, reconstituted the college as one of eight secular priests, with one Gilbert Bowet as Master. Six chantries were established, dedicated respectively to St. Mary, St. Andrew, St. John the Baptist, St. Thomas of Canterbury, St. Katharine and St. Peter. Reminders of these chantry chapels are the piscina drains at the east end of the south and north aisles. The chantry at the eastern end of the south aisle was that dedicated to our Lady, and it has happily been again furnished with an altar as a memorial to Greystoke men who fell in the 1939–45 war. During Easter-tide an "Easter Garden" and at Christmas a Crib are placed near to this altar, the whole effect providing a focus of attention and devotion which is sadly missing where a wide aisle ends in a blank wall or a confusion of pews.

Further evidences of the church's former collegiate status are the well-preserved return-end oak stalls in the chancel, with their carved misericord seats. The sedilia in the sanctuary were reconstructed in 1848, but much of the original stonework was used again.

The visitor to this fine church should notice the late Perpendicular screen in which is incorporated the ancient Rood beam (perhaps one day to bear again the crucified figure of the Saviour of men), the mediaeval glass in the ancient east window, various memorial brasses in the chancel and elsewhere, the priest's chamber with its 15th century fireplace, and the southward tilt of the 13th century chancel arch. This is actually the oldest part of the building and its bias is sometimes attributed to the former existence of a central

---

*Known as *le bon baron*—the "good" lord.

tower, said to have been destroyed by the raiding Scots during the feeble regime of Edward II. Be that as it may, the present tower at the west end of the church was probably not built until the 15th century and was entirely reconstructed some time after 1840.

It seems almost certain that originally the church had not only a central tower, but north and south transepts, making it a cruciform building. Narrow, "lean-to" aisles would flank the five-arched nave. The original piers of the nave arcade seem to have been replaced, at some period difficult to determine, by plain, round columns. The arches are said to have been heightened somewhat when some interior alterations were made to the building in 1817–18. The present north and south aisles, with their outside walls, the sacristy, priest's chamber and south porch, all date from the 15th century. These enlargements were carried out presumably to provide greater space for the six chantries.

Near the organ are the remains of a piscina, indicating the position of one of the chantry altars, and near to it is visual evidence of a now walled-up staircase which once provided access to the rood loft. In mediaeval times it was customary to sing the Gospel at High Mass from the rood loft on certain festivals.

This splendid parish church, surprisingly large for so small a village —even allowing for the propinquity of Greystoke Castle—should not be missed by the lover of antiquity and of the Border counties. Standing as it does amid lush green pastures and at the end of a straight approach which is half village street and half country lane, it breathes the true spirit of Cumbria's stirring past and worthily enshrines the memories of bygone Howards, Haltons, Dacres, Grimthorpes, Hudlestons, Dowsons and Askews.

There are several interesting monuments and memorial windows in Greystoke Church. The window over the priest's door on the south side of the chancel contains nine lozenges in ancient glass with the device of the Blessed Trinity in its centre and in other parts quaint symbolic figures with the legend, "cantemus duo glorose, mo . . . nante, lape, nas . . . finis" and *Osanna* several times repeated.

In the chancel there is also a window in memory of Henry Howard of Greystoke (d. 1875), nephew of Bernard Edward, twelfth Duke of Norfolk, and another in memory of Henry Askew, rector of Greystoke for 54 years. These two were conjointly responsible for the restoration, in 1848, of the splendid east window which contains all that remains of the church's mediaeval glass. Some of this had been removed from the church in 1790 and placed in the chapel of Greystoke Castle. The upper half of the window contains a miscellaneous collection of fragments of very early glass, arranged as far as possible to give a pleasing colour effect. In the lower part of the five main lights some 15th century fragments present a more consecutive and coherent series of pictures depicting incidents from the legendary life of St. Andrew. In one of the main lights the saint is depicted trampling upon a scarlet and prostrate devil. The upper lights and tracery were filled with 19th century glass of heraldic devices showing the royal arms, those of the diocese of Carlisle, the Howard crosslets, the Dacre scallop shell and the Askew crest.

The window above the sedilia on the south side of the sanctuary displays the arms of the ancient families formerly connected with Greystoke—Hutton of Hutton John; Blencowe of Blencowe Hall; Threlkeld of Threlkeld Hall; Pickering of Threlkeld; Halton of Greenthwaite Hall; Dalston of Thwaite Hall; Musgrave, Wyvill and Williams of Johnby Hall. Other windows in the church are in memory of various members of the Hudleston family of Hutton John, of Dowsons of Lattendales and of Rileys of Ennim.

On the south side of the chancel arch is a memorial to a former occupant and owner of Johnby Hall:

"Guilielmus Williams de St. Nicola in comitatu Glamorgan, Generosus (toga sumpta virili) sub signis Car. I.R.A. constanter militavit. Dein lapsis aliquot annis, Cumbriam auspicato veriens, ingessit se curis tam diu fraterno consilio prospere euntibus, quam mox turbidis, quorumdam livore. Dicitur sibi interea uxor Barbara charissima pia. His, quatuor filialibus (intercisis aliquot) beatus, postquam domi biennium morbo contabuit, charus amicis, Deo animam pie concessit (cunctis suis moerentibus) 12th Januarii, A.D. 1679."

The south wall of the nave bears memorial tablets to:

(i) John Dowson, d. 24th October 1771, and Anne his wife. Also their son, William Dowson, D.D., Principal of St. Edmund Hall, Oxford, who died 9th Jan., 1800.

(ii) Barbara, wife of William Irving, surgeon, of Hesket New Market, who died Dec. 9th, 1812, aet. 57.

(iii) Capt. Thos. Nayler, R. Marines, who died at Ennom Bank, near Blencowe, Aug. 6, 1802, aet. 44, and his two wives— Mary Grimshaw of Preston and Elizabeth Dalton of Thurnham Hall, both in Co. Lancs.

(iv) Sally Mounsey, daughter of Sarah Mounsey (and wife of William Sanderson) d. 10 Mar. 1812, aet. 25; erected by her brother, Rev. Thos. Mounsey of Stamford, Lincs.

(v) A white marble monument to George Calvert, who died at at Greystoke Castle, 1 Nov. 1770, aged 70, son of James Calvert, late of Ferry Bridge, co. York. This George Calvert was factor to the Duke of Norfolk and uncle to Wordsworth's friend and benefactor, Raisley Calvert of Windebrowe, Keswick, who was baptised at Greystoke in 1773 and buried there in 1795.

(vi) A large marble monument in the west wall of the south aisle proclaims:
> "Hic jacet Alanus Smalwood, S.T.P.,
> Ecclesiae hujusce Rect: Obiit 15 Octob.
> A.D. 1686, aetat 79."

There are several interesting brasses to be seen. One near the vestry door, on the floor of the south aisle, reads:
> Milo Haltonus LVII an
> natus adsessor comita
> tus Cumbr Eiusdemq vi
> cecomes X Liberis Bea
> tus curis reip famili
> aeq. Pressus Perpetuum
> utriq. Dediserandus Tr
> ansistus exemplum praebuit.
> XVII. Kal. Ap. CI CLII

The two alabaster figures of knights, now placed at the west end of the south aisle, were probably originally recumbent upon tombs in a recess on the north side of the choir. The smaller effigy, which is similar to one of Sir John de Herteshull at Ashton, Northants, wears armour very like that worn by the Black Prince at Poitiers and now preserved over his tomb in Canterbury Cathedral (c. 1376). This effigy probably represents William, "le bon Baron de Graistok." The larger figure, broken off at the knees, represents John, 16th Baron Graystock, who married Elizabeth, daughter and heiress of

Robert, Baron Ferrers of Wemme. By his Will, dated 10 July, 1436, he ordered his body to be buried in the collegiate church of Graystock, and bequeathed to that church "his best horse as a mortuary, and all his habiliments of war, consisting of coat armour, pennon, gyron, etc."

The priest's chamber, now used as a vestry, probably contained an altar. There is a piscina on the south wall, and on an inner wall a fine 15th century fireplace. A stone spiral staircase leads to a room overhead, once no doubt occupied by a member of the mediaeval college, possibly by the priest responsible for the duties of sacristan.

The ancient collegiate character of Greystoke church has been in a measure restored to it by the inauguration, in 1958, of a scheme for assisting young men with a vocation to the ministry of the Church to acquire the academic qualifications required for admission to a theological college. About a dozen such postulants live in lodgings in the village, attend lectures given by a panel of mostly voluntary tutors, and study under the supervision of the Rector, who is Warden of the College, and of a chaplain-tutor. Each day the Offices of Mattins and Evensong are recited corporately, the clergy and students sitting in the choir stalls once occupied for a similar purpose by their mediaeval predecessors. In this way is revived something of the former nature of the worship offered within the walls of this ancient church, linking its hallowed and historic past with the spiritual and ecclesiastical needs of the present. The Greystoke experiment is not the least interesting and possibly not the least useful of the ways by which the Church's need for more priests is being met.

At the Dissolution of the Monasteries in the reign of Henry VIII chantries as such ceased to exist and, like other collegiate foundations, Greystoke reverted to its former purely parochial status under a Rector. The earliest recorded name of a Rector of Greystoke is that of Thomas de Vipont (who was ultimately consecrated Bishop of Carlisle in 1255). In 1357, as we have seen *Richard de Hoton Roof* became Rector. Hutton Roof*, a hamlet seven miles from Greystoke, is still a part of this widely-scattered parish and there is maintained a Church of England Primary School receiving children from a wide area.

*Richard, however, possibly hailed from the other Hutton Roof, in south Westmorland.

Gilbert Bowet has already been mentioned as Rector in 1382, and he is described in the Register of Bishop Appleby as *Magister sive Custos Collegii perpetui de Graystock*. John Whelpdale, L.L.D. was a native of Greystoke who became Rector of the parish and master of the College. He died in 1526 and there is an armorial brass to his memory under the modern choir seats in the south transept, near the altar of our Lady.

The last Master of the College, John Dacre, L.L.B. (1537–1567), held the Rectory of Greystoke in conjunction with that of Wem in Shropshire. "He conformed to all the ritual changes during the first years of Queen Elizabeth, and died in 1567." (Carlisle Episcopal Registers; Best; fol. 22.) Five stones in the north wall of the chancel are inscribed: "I.D.P.G. Ao.Di. 1557"—P.G. standing either for "Provost of Greystoke" (during Queen Mary's brief reign) or *Ponendum curaverunt*, in which case the "G" is really a "C"!

William Morland, M.A. (1640–1663) was presented to the benefice by Thomas Howard, Earl of Arundel and Surrey who, in partnership with Morland, restored the chancel in 1645—an act of piety commemorated at the foot of the east window. During the period of the Commonwealth the living was sequestrated by order of Sir Arthur Hazelrigg, the Cromwellian Commissioner for the Northern Counties, on the grounds of "ignorance and insufficiency," but Morland was reinstated at the Restoration in 1660.

Thomas Gibbon, D.D. (1693–1716) was appointed Dean of Carlisle in 1712. He it was who rebuilt the handsome Rectory (the "old Rectory," as it now is) in 1702, presented a silver chalice and paten to the church, and erected a sundial which may still be seen on the stone "alms-table" on the south side of the churchyard.

Edmund Law, D.D. (1739–1788) had been Master of St. Peter's College, Cambridge. He was consecrated Bishop of Carlisle in 1768, after having held the livings of Greystoke and Great Salkeld in plurality. He was the father of the first Lord Ellenborough (Lord Chief Justice of England 1802–1818) and of two other sons, both of whom became bishops.

During the long incumbency of Henry Askew, M.A. (1798–1850), the tower was re-built in 1848 and the east window was restored in conjunction with Mr. Henry Howard of Greystoke Castle. His grandson, Edmund Adam Askew, was Rector of Greystoke from 1875 to 1901 and an honorary Canon of Carlisle. The fine organ was presented by members of the Howard family in 1899, and the Chapel-of-Ease (All Saints') at Penruddock was consecrated by Bishop Bardsley in 1901.

There is a list of all the incumbents of Greystoke down to the present day to be seen on the inner west wall of the nave, near to the tower entrance. The figure of our Lady and the Holy Child was carved during the war by a German prisoner-of-war, one of those encamped within the walls of Greystoke Castle. It was carved from a single piece of yew wood and presented to the church in 1945. The very fine plaster *Crucifixus* on the west wall of the south aisle is the work of the well-known sculptor, Josephina de Vasconcellos. It was commissioned by Sir Kenneth Grubb and is on permanent loan to Greystoke Church. The ancient Muniments "Kist," with its customary triple locks, dates from Elizabethan times and originally housed the Parish Registers. These are now kept for safety in the County Archives at Carlisle.

The old, moss-grown sundial mentioned above, which is to be seen standing on a large stone Alms Table by the path leading through the south side of the churchyard, bears the date 1710. It was erected, as already stated, by the Reverend Thomas Gibbon, Rector at that time, and is a sixteen-inch cube. It appears originally to have had a surmounting ornament of some kind, since the iron clamp pins for such an addition still remain.

On the east face of the dial appear the words *Lux Est* ("It is light"); on the south face, the single word *Redime* ("Redeem"); on the west face, *Nox Venit* ("the Night cometh"), and on the back and north side is inscribed

GRAYSTOCK, LAT. 54° 46″, T.G. MDCCX.

The Alms Table would be used for the annual distribution, in cash or in kind, of various charitable gifts bequeathed for the good of the poor of the parish by sundry pious benefactors.

The attention of visitors entering or leaving the church is drawn to the mediaeval Sanctuary Stone which now stands about a hundred yards from the church gates, protected by a wrought-iron grille. It formerly stood in the middle of the causeway leading to the church and is said to have marked the boundary beyond which fugitives from justice could claim "sanctuary" and the protection of the Church. It can be seen on the right-hand side of the lane as one goes towards the village.

GREYSTOKE PARISH REGISTERS

ANCIENT parish registers can be rich sources of historical information and, not infrequently, of considerable quiet amusement. They can also be the cause of occasional irritation, as when some well-meaning but thoughtless person arrives on the rectory door-step fifteen minutes before a service is due to begin and requests a search for family names going back possibly two hundred years. They would like the information at once, please, because they are catching a ship bound for the Antipodes the following morning!

St. Andrew's church, Greystoke, has a printed edition of its registers between the years 1559 and 1757. These entries were compiled and published by a former rector, the Reverend A. M. Maclean, in 1911, and they throw an interesting light on many aspects of church and village life in bygone days. The earlier entries tend to be brief and somewhat repetitious. The Elizabethan parish clergy were usually poorly educated and no doubt found literary composition an onerous task. As we should expect, the spelling is frequently eccentric and inconsistent; the English language was still in the process of formation and orthography was largely a matter of individual preference. Surnames, not surprisingly, show a strong tendency to recur over long periods. Although Greystoke was not isolated in the sense that some of the dales parishes were, there was of course a far greater tendency than nowadays for families in the 17th and 18th centuries to continue to be domiciled in the same place for several successive generations. They seem to have had little of the restlessness of their modern counterparts and in any case far less opportunity for indulging it. There was much intermarrying between families, and clearly a good deal of laxity in certain cases in the matter of pre-marital and post-marital fidelity. A certain number of couples over the period in question appear to have dispensed entirely with nuptial formalities of any ecclesiastical or legal kind.

Many of the entries reflect happenings of a local or more general nature. Against the date March 3rd, 1576, for example, we find this entry: "Buried—a straung (i.e. strange) woman which died

Levens Hall

The Topiary, Levens Hall

at Penruddock, suspected to come from the Dutchmen." This cryptic remark refers, of course, to the German (Deutsch) miners settled in the Keswick area to work the Newlands copper mines. What connection this unfortunate woman had had with them one can only surmise.

Death on the roads was no doubt far rarer than in our time, but tragedy found other ways of claiming its victims as entries such as these remind us:

> "1578 4th July—Buried Willm son of Robert Murray's wiffe, widow, wch was drowned in the Hall well (which Hall?), being of the aige of 14 years."

> "1587 12th November—Buried Margaret Lancaster, a poore childe wch went for God's Sake."

> "1594 22nd July—Buried Elizabeth Parker, widow, wch drowned herselfe in the Hall well at Johnbye."

> "1597 18th June—Buried a poor man wch died upon the pasture a little from Jacks wiffes of Beryer."*

> "1598/9 17th February—Buried Robert Rumney, a pore man of G(raistock) wch was found lying dead upon Newbigin pasture in the Highe Streat a little from Fluskay." (Flusco)†

> "1623 27th March—Buried a poore hungersterven beger child— Dorethy d. of Henry Patteson, miller."

(Many "poore begers," etc., are recorded as being buried in this particular year, which may have been a year of crop failure and therefore of widespread famine.)

> "1742 5th August—Buried John Nicholson, a Servant of Thomas Capes of Berriar, who was unfortunately killed by reason of a Horse running away with a Cart—Ye sd Jno born at G(reystoke)."

A reminder from one of the earlier entries of the prevailing general illiteracy is provided on:

> "1578/9 5th March—Buried John Clemetson of G. called 'The Scholler';"

---

*Berrier is a hamlet about three miles from Greystoke.
†Flusco is near Blencowe railway station, in the parish of Dacre.

Brougham Castle and the river Eamont
The Countess's Pillar, Brougham

and of the prevalence of a certain degree of moral indifference in such entries as:

> "1578/9 6th January—Christened Agnes d. of Lancillote Halton and Margaret Chamers his concupyne."

> "1588/9 9th February—Wedded John Robinson of Grysdell (Mungrisdale)—wright—and Agnes Todhunter of the same and did acknowledge their offence because the woman was wth child."

One of the most remarkable incumbents of Greystoke was Dr. Alan Smallwood, who was Rector from 1663 until 1686. In contrast to the laconic entries of most of his predecessors, this worthy divine was apt to record his ministrations in verse, some of it distinctly more pungent than a modern archdeacon would see fit to approve. For example:

> "1677 12th August—Christened:
> This day Baptizd a child Immanuell
> Soe called, but who's his father few can tell
> Some say John Hall, because his wife's ye mother,
> But many censure that he is another.
> Who e'er he be, let him that needs enquire.
> I think he sprang not from a Godly Scire
> Cornutus est, who for his long absence
> Gives not his wife her due benevolence."

Other entries from the same reverend pen are couched in even more forthright terms. Seventeenth-century laws of libel clearly did not extend to what was written in parochial registers.

Many of the entries give us glimpses of ecclesiastical customs and arrangements. We read, for example, of a new incumbent towards the end of Queen Elizabeth's reign:

> "1597 19th June. Sunday the nineteenth day was Mr. Leonard Lowther inducted P'son of Graistocke and did make one sermon upon the thirteenth chapter to the Hebrues, seventeenth verse, 'Obey them that have the oversight of you' (a not very tactful choice of text, perhaps, in the circumstances!), and he did read the Articles set furth by the Archbyshopp and byshopps by the Queenes Matye Aucthoritie in the presence of the whole p(ar)ishe then there assembled."

The marriage of a brother cleric, a member of a noted local family, was solemnized a few months later, presumably by the said Mr. Leonard Lowther, and is of interest as indicating that the old mediaeval custom of addressing a priest as "Sir" had not yet entirely died out.

"1597/8 19th February. Wedded Sr Robert Troutbeck—clerck— and Grace Clematson, both of Great Blencow in the p(ar)ishe of Dacre and they had a lycense from Mr. Chancellor dated the 5th of Februarie."

Then there were great days when the parish was honoured with a visitation from its ecclesiastical superior.

"1604 16th September—Was the Right Reverend Fayther Henrye by God's Dyvin prydence Busshope of Carlill at Graystock Church and dyd preche: Matt. 6, 33 verse."

A year later we find a sidelight on current sacramental practice.

"1605 4th August—A Generall Communion and Mr. Person (parson) dyd mynistr in his owne person (was the pun intentional?), Mr. Leonard Musgrave, Mr. Henry Blencowe, wth men, wiffs, and younge folke, the most part dyd receave the same daye. Mrs. Isabell Musgrave and Mrs. Eleanor Musgrave, daughter of Mr. Leonard Musgrave, was at Dyvine Service and Sermon, and all other his servants beinge recusants."

This enumeration of the "quality" present at the service was not snobbery on the part of "Mr. Person." These were the times of the savage penal laws directed against Romanist recusants, when failure on the part of the latter to attend divine service in their parish church might well involve them in a swingeing fine. "Mr. Person's" recording of the Musgraves' presence at his service was their protection against the rigours of the law.

The ancient parish of Greystoke, served as it was by a college of priests (dissolved at the Reformation), included the villages of Mungrisdale, Threlkeld, Matterdale and Watermillock. These all became separate parishes in the course of the 19th century, as they are to this day. To mark this ancient connection the "daughter" parishes make pilgrimage to their "mother church" of Greystoke annually on the fourth Sunday in Lent—commonly known as

"Mothering Sunday." A similar kind of filial affection on the part of the daughters seems to have existed in the year of the Gunpowder Plot, though they had not yet achieved an independent parochial existence of their own.

> "November 13th, 1605.—Sundaye was at the Church (Greystoke) the most part of the p(ar)ishioners men and wiffs and the Curats at Waltermelock, Matterdayle and Grysdell, and Mr. Parson dyd ministr the whole Service in his own person and dyd preche forenone and aftr none two sermons."

Four years later the Register was recording events of varying solemnity.

> "1609. 13th August—Was the Right Reverend Fayther Henrye by God's Dyvine Prydence Bishope of Carlisle at Graistock Church and dyd preche . . . and this same daye was the Honorable the Lady Anne (née Dacre) Countess of Arundell at Graistock Castell, the Lord Wyllm Howard and the Lady Elizabethe his wiffe with many other straingers. My Ld. Byshoppe dyd dine there and after evening prayer at Church dyd conffyrme a greate number of children."

By now, it would seem, the recusants had become less amenable, the penal laws having been for some time less stringently enforced.

> "1609, 30th November—Was openly pronounced an Excommunication against Mr. Joseph Hudleston, Elynor his wife, Wynefryde Musgrave widow, Isabele Musgrave, George Mounsey, Joan his wife—as is thought by certayn"—

an unkind touch, this last, one would have thought!

But perhaps the excommunicated detected the workings of divine justice four days later.

> "3rd December—Buried, Mr. Leonard Lowther parson of Graystock and Lowther, wch Mr. Lowther departed to the mercye of God the same day and was buried at Lowther Church."

Two months later the parish was further bereaved.

> "1609/10 31st January—Wednesday was buried Sir Willm Smythson curate, which served at this Church as curate two and fyftie yeeres last past."

An entry made during the next reign, that of King Charles I, records a further item of local historical interest.

"1634 27th December—Buried Randall Dacre Esq., son and Heyre to Francis Dacre, deceased, being the youngest son of the late Lord Willm Dacre, deceased, being the last heyre male of that lyne, wch sd Randall dyed at London and was brought down at the charge of the Right Hoble Thomas Earle of Arundell and Surreye and Earl Marshal of England."

Excommunicated or not, "Mr. Joseph Huddleston Esq." (sic) of Hutton John, who died in November 1646, was not denied burial "*in the church*," a privilege for which the fee was fixed two years later at five shillings. It is not clear whether that other ex-communicated recusant, Mrs. Wynefrede Musgrave of Johnby Hall was accorded a similar funerary privilege when she died on the 5th March, 1656—"an ancient old woman" is how the Register somewhat unchivalrously describes her. Perhaps her relations at Johnby were not prepared to expend five shillings that she might enjoy the privilege of burial within a church wherein they them-selves no longer worshipped.

In 1661 we find mention of special collections being made in the parish for various deserving outside causes.

"*Imprimis.* For the rebuilding of the Church of Pontefracte collected in the whole p(ar)ishe the summe of nyneteen shillings and two pence halfe penny.

Item. For the poore Inhabitants of Great Drayton in the County of Salop the summe of fifteen shillings and foure pence in the whole p(ar)ishe.

Item. For the Inhabitants of the great Dukedowm of Lithuania the summe of three shillings and sixe pence (in this Church).

Item. For Scarborrow Church the summe of four shillings and two pence (in this Church).

1666. Payde in to William Ritson ye Recever for ye Ld Bsp of Carlile the summe of fifty eight shillings being ye Collection within ye whole Parrish for ye distressed people in and about London, who were undone by ye late dreadfull Fire Nov. ye 2nd last past."

In view of these varied benefactions no one could accuse the Greystoke people of the Restoration period of being narrowly parochial or unmindful of the wider claims of their fellow Christians upon their interest and generosity. It will, of course, be remembered that a shilling in the reign of King Charles II represented a day's wage for a farm worker, and was roughiy equivalent to about ten shillings of our money.

In 1665, the year of the great London Plague, the Reverend Dr. Smallwood was already Rector of Greystoke, and we are entering upon the period of more copious (and, as I have said, often more scurrilous) entries in the Registers. On the 22nd October of that year for example, there is recorded a marriage with an authentic Darby and Joan flavour. No brief factual entry sufficed in this case.

> "What time brings forth there's none that can presage./ John Todhunter, of Eighty Year of Age,/ Wed to Anne Strickatt, who's supposed to be/ a Virgin and her age is Sixty-Three./ Both of this parrish, wch causes Admiration./ The like has scarce been knowne wthin this station."

Correctly scanned, the facts recorded in the above remarkable entry can be seen to have inspired the good Doctor's poetic muse.

There are frequent entries in the Registers recording the baptisms of those "of riper years" who were of Quaker origin and so had not been brought to the font in infancy. A typical example is to be found in 1682:

> "12th January. Christened Agnes the daughter of Thomas Slee of Hutton John (being about Twentye years old). She was not baptized in her infancy by reason of her parents' Profession (i.e., religious persuasion), who were then Quakers."

Perhaps we may conclude with an account of another noteworthy wedding mentioned by the Reverend A. M. Maclean in his published extracts from the Greystoke Registers. It was printed in *The Star* for the 30th May, 1704:

> "A marriage, rather singular in some circumstances, was celebrated at Greystoke Church, in the county of Cumberland, a few days ago, when Mr. John Peacock of Redsyke led the agreeable widow Scott to the altar. It was the fourth visit

the lady had made on such occasions. They were attended by an *old* acquaintance, in the capacity of the bridegroom's man, whose age, being added to the ages of the happy couple, produced the sum of 230 years! The lady was carried to to church by another old acquaintance—a horse, which had twice performed the same kind of office for her, and who is now in his thirty-sixth year. The ceremony was conducted with great sobriety, the party having prudently determined not to suffer their domestic felicity to be interrupted by any visitors whatever."

And as a final footnote from the Churchwardens' Accounts for 1746/7:

"To ye ringers at a Rejoicing for a victory over ye Rebels at Culloddon. April ye 16, 1746—1s. 6d.

For hiding the Church Plate 2 several times when the Rebels came out of Scoteland,—1s. 0d."

EAGLESFIELD'S FAME

NOT far from Cockermouth, on Lakeland's northern fringe, is the village of Eaglesfield which has more than one claim to fame. Its oldest, perhaps, is the fact that it was the birthplace of Robert of Eglesfield, chaplain to Queen Philippa, wife of Edward III. It was Robert who persuaded Philippa to found Queen's College, Oxford, and it was at his prompting decreed that preference should always be given at Queen's to students from the counties of Cumberland and Westmorland. A close connection between the college and the Lakeland counties continues to exist.

John Dalton, the chemist, was born in a cottage at Eaglesfield in 1766. He is not to be confused with the other John Dalton, poet and divine who, strangely enough, was born only a few miles away, at Dean Vicarage, in 1709. A plaque upon the wall of the cottage at Eaglesfield commemorates the Cumbrian who became so famous a man of science.

Although born and bred in Cumberland, Dalton's highest achievements belong to Kendal and Manchester. Nevertheless he had his earliest triumphs here at Eaglesfield where at a tender age, being no more than ten years old, he foreshadowed his future fame and gave evidence of a mathematical precocity by constructing an almanac of considerable ingenuity. At the age of thirteen, having presumably exhausted all that was available locally in the way of formal education, he set up as a schoolmaster on his own account, painting over the doorway of his one-roomed village academy, "Pens, Ink and Paper sold here." When one thinks of some of the products of our modern, fantastically expensive, State-provided schooling who, at the age that Dalton was then, can scarcely write a sentence of tolerable English—but I must not be tempted to digress into such melancholy musings.

In 1781, at the age of fifteen, young Dalton removed to Kendal to become assistant to his cousin Jonathan who was an assistant master at the Quaker School in that town. Four years later the two Daltons succeeded George Bewley as principals of the school, John in the meantime having progressed rapidly in his studies of the natural sciences under the guidance of John Gough, known as the Blind Philosopher. At Gough's suggestion Dalton began in Kendal his meteorological journal. This was in 1789, and he kept it assiduously and methodically for fifty-seven years, by the end of which time it contained something like 200,000 observations. In conjunction with his friend Peter Crosthwaite of Keswick, Dalton was able to make many valuable discoveries and gain for himself a European reputation in the fields of chemistry, botany and meteorology. As lecturer in Mathematics and Physical Science at New College, Manchester, Dalton was the recipient of a number of awards from both British and foreign learned scientific societies.

His fame was vastly increased when, in 1808, he published his *New System of Chemical Philosophy*, and continued to blossom until his death in 1844. Eleven years before he died his statue in marble, the work of the most famous sculptor of the day, Sir Francis Chantrey, was placed at the entrance of the Royal Institution in Manchester. Yet success never turned his head or modified his homely Cumbrian speech. In 1835, he was presented to King William IV, and when that monarch asked him how he was getting on in Manchester, Dalton is reputed to have replied, "Well, I don't know; just middlin', I think." Some friends later chided him over his want of polish, protesting that in so addressing his Sovereign he had not exactly exhibited Court manners. "Mebbe not," replied Dalton, "but what can ye say tae sic like fowk?"

A curious thing about John Dalton was that he was colour-blind. As a youth in Kendal he purchased for his mother a pair of silken hose for her to wear to the Meeting House on the Lord's Day. Delighted though she was her son's thoughtfulness, the good Quaker dame was thrown into a state of great alarm by the colour of the stockings. They were of bright scarlet, though Dalton had bought what to him looked like articles of the most sombre drab.

Of his own minor disability John Dalton wrote in 1794, "The flowers of most of the cranes-bills which others call pink appear to me in the day almost exactly sky-blue; while others call them deep pink; but happening once to look at one in the night by candle-light, I found it of a colour as different as possible from daylight. It seemed then near yellow, but with a tincture of red; whilst nobody else said it differed from its daylight appearance, my brother excepted, who seems to see as I do."* As a good scientist, Dalton turned his peculiarity to good account by basing upon it a detailed study of the phenomenon of colour and colour-blindness.

Dalton never married though he once confessed to his old Eaglesfield friend and mentor, Elihu Robinson, that on one occasion he had come near to it. The young lady who thus temporarily captivated him would appear to have been a fellow-student, or possibly a pupil. She was clearly a "blue-stocking" in whatever shade of the spectrum her charms presented themselves to the colour-blind Dalton. "She descanted to me upon the use of dephlogisticated marine acid in bleaching and upon the effects of opium in the animal system. During my captivity, which lasted about a week, I lost my appetite and had other symptoms of bondage about me, but have now happily regained my freedom."† The truth was that he was too absorbed in his work, too dedicated in his pursuit of fresh discoveries, to spare the time for such irrelevancies as courtship and matrimony.

Eaglesfield has every reason to feel proud of its home-produced, largely self-taught genius. One wonders how he would have fared under the more stereotyped education systems of later times. No doubt the paths of learning would have been smoothed for him in his earlier years. He would certainly not have found himself in charge of the village school at the age of thirteen, nor assistant usher of a quasi-technical college two years later. Nor, indeed, without the regulation credentials inscribed on parchment or the necessary appendage of coloured silk upon his back, could he have risen to the academic heights he subsequently achieved. But, since genius formulates its own standards and requirements, it need not be doubted that John Dalton of Eaglesfield would have been heard of and acclaimed, even in an age as deferential as our own to the more conventional methods of measuring and assessing intellectual ability and worth.

*   *   *   *

On the Cockermouth side of Eaglesfield is Moorland Close, with its arched entrance to the farmyard and famous as the birthplace of Fletcher Christian. To cinema-goers of a past generation this name

---

*A Bag of Old Letters, by John Dalton, p. 85.
†Ibid, p. 87.

will conjure up memories of the film, *Mutiny on the Bounty;* perhaps of the scene in which the late Charles Laughton, as Captain Bligh, R.N., confronts his first officer, Fletcher Christian, on the quarter-deck of his ship and, after listening to a recital of the crew's demands, rasps in those deliberate, contemptuous tones which characterised his superb performance, "This—is—*mutiny*—Mr. Christian!"

Whether Captain Bligh was in fact the ruthless tyrant depicted in the film, and whether the mutineers led by Lieutenant Fletcher Christian were justified in the charges they levelled against him, has been a subject for debate from that day to this. The facts themselves, however, are not in question.

H.M.S. *Bounty* was sent by the Admiralty, in 1787, to Tahiti to collect plants of the bread fruit tree for cultivation in the West Indies. On the return voyage, after sampling the lotus-eating delights of Tahiti, the crew led by Fletcher Christian mutinied and set Bligh and a few seamen who were loyal to him adrift in an open boat. After an epic voyage of intense privation and as a result of Bligh's superb seamanship, he and his men finally reached Timor across 4,000 miles of ocean, returning to England in 1790.

As for the mutineers, some returned to Tahiti and settled there, only to be found by a naval vessel sent to apprehend them and shipped back to England for trial and sentence. The rest, led by that canny Cumbrian Fletcher Christian, sailed for the bleak remoteness of Pitcairn Island where their descendants continue to this day. The present writer, voyaging as a child to New Zealand, recollects the ship anchoring off this far-from-inviting looking island, which appeared to consist for the most part of a towering volcanic peak, its summit shrouded in clouds of mist. Through the surf thundering against the shores, parties of islanders came off in boats with fruit and curios made from sea-shells, coral and the feathers of exotically-coloured birds. These they traded in exchange for articles otherwise unobtainable by them such as second-hand clothes, shoes, tools, cutlery and so forth. Had I known then the full drama of the story which had led to the existence of these swarthy islanders, with their odd assortment of tattered garments, I should no doubt have paid more attention to their appearance and their speech than to the miscellaneous wares which they spread upon the decks of the good ship *Remuera*.

Little enough, then, is known for certain of Fletcher Christian of Moorland Close and the famous Mutiny which he led in the year that saw the fall of the Bastille and the beginnings of an upheaval of drastically greater significance for Europe and mankind. But where history has been sparing speculation, as so often, has been more liberal. Sir John Barrow, an Ulverston man, wrote, in 1831, *The Eventful History of the Mutiny of H.M.S. Bounty*, and in it tells circumstantially how one Heywood, a midshipman who had sided with the mutineers, had been condemned at the court-martial but subsequently pardoned. This Heywood claimed that in 1808 or 1809 he saw at dusk in one of the back streets of Plymouth a figure which he recognized, or claimed to recognize, as that of Fletcher Christian. At about this time there were strong rumours of Christian's having been seen in and around the Lake District.

Out of such dubious hear-say some more recent writers, notably Mr. C. S. Wilkinson,* have woven fascinating if inconclusive theories concerning the ex-mutineer and his alleged secret return to his native land, where the gallows almost certainly awaited him should he have been recognized and apprehended. Mr. Wilkinson rightly reminds us that for a brief period between 1775 and 1779 Christian and William Wordsworth were fellow-pupils at the old Grammar School at Cockermouth. It is also known that Edward Christian, Fletcher's elder brother and a man versed in law, had collected a number of sworn statements from sundry witnesses at the Court-martial, all purporting to attest his brother's innocence of complicity in the mutiny. Among those who were present when these witnesses gave their testimony and signed attestations to the truth of the transcripts of those testimonies, were several of Wordsworth's relations, his former college tutor at Cambridge and three of his personal friends. On these perhaps not very substantial threads Mr. Wilkinson suspends his theories—that in 1795 Wordsworth and Fletcher Christian met somewhere in Bristol, that Wordsworth concealed his fellow-Cumbrian at Nether Stowey where Coleridge was living at the time, and later smuggled him away to safety in the North, perhaps to Dumfriesshire where there were numerous connections of the Christian family. It is a romantic and interesting theory, but the thread of fact upon which it all depends seems a slender one for so weighty a load of supposition.

*In *The Wake of the Bounty*, London, 1953.

Yet the story of Fletcher Christian, however dubious the light it sheds upon this former Cockermouth schoolboy, is a romantic enough tale in its own right and will always have its place in the annals of Cumberland.

*   *   *   *

There are other houses of interest within no great distance of Eaglesfield. Isel Hall, the ancient home of the Lawson family, is an Elizabethan extension of an earlier pele-tower; Hewthwaite Hall has an inscription over its doorway recording that "John Swynburn and his wyf did make cost of this work in the dais of their lyfe. 1581;" and in Setmurthy village, between Isel and Bassenthwaite Lake, was the school, since demolished, where Thomas Farrell, author of the famous dialect stories known as *Betty Wilson's Cummerlan' Teals*, was master. Vicar of this parish from 1842 until 1850 was the Reverend Charles Southey, son of the Poet Laureate. And also in this neighbourhood, between Broughton and Dearham, is the house known as Whistling Syke, built in 1708 by the grandfather of the famous Josiah Wedgwood. Earthenware was manufactured here long before the Etruria works took shape and helped to transform rural Staffordshire into the Black Country. So once more it was Cumbrian skill and enterprise which paved the way for one of Britain's most renowned and most profitable industries.

On a slightly less material note, mention should be made of Pardshaw Crag, a mile or two to the south of Eaglesfield. Here, in 1663, George Fox preached to an audience estimated to exceed ten thousand, the peculiar formation of this limestone outcrop providing both natural open-air pulpit and acoustics which enabled the preacher's voice to carry to the utmost edges of a crowd even of those vast proportions. Many a modern preacher would gladly settle for a congregation of half that number, and approximately half that number, so we are told, confronted the American revivalist and temperance reformer, Neale Dow, when he preached from Pardshaw Crag in 1857. It is said that the occasion was rendered memorable by reason of the amount of beer sold and consumed, but whether this is to be accounted for by the excessive heat of the day or because of a desire for a final fling before the pledge was taken, history does not reveal.

TWO STATELY HOMES

MUCH of the history of a country, of a locality, is written in stone—or in bricks and mortar. Farmsteads, cottages, town houses, castles, noble mansions—all have something to tell of past ages, of former inhabitants and their way of life. And of course the greater the house and the longer its lineage the more, in all probability, it has to reveal.

Westmorland's history, for instance, is enhanced and underlined by the existence of two stately houses of considerable antiquity, both of them within easy reach of Kendal, the county administrative centre. These are Sizergh Castle and Levens Hall. Both are open to the public at specified times, yet both are lived in and are homes. The fact that these two houses are lived in still is, I think, of particular importance. An undwelt-in house, however beautiful its architecture, however romantic its setting or stirring its record and however rich its contents, can seldom avoid an air of something lacking. A museum-like atmosphere tends to pervade it. Missing, as a rule, are the personal touches, the sense of intimacy and affection imparted by freshly-arranged flowers, the family photographs and the small personal possessions left casually lying here and there which speak of present human occupation. One may have paid one's entrance fee at the door and be conducted around by a knowledgeable and well-trained guide. But it is far more heart-warming to feel that one is privileged to walk around someone's home, to realise that what one is looking at are cherished belongings and not merely *objets d'art* or items of antiquarian interest.

At Sizergh it is quite on the cards that one will be shown around by the present occupier, and former owner, of the castle in person. When Mr. Henry Hornyhold married the eldest daughter of the late Baron Strickland (some-time Prime Minister of Malta) who had no male heir, he assumed the surname of Strickland in addition to his own in order to ensure the continuity of a family which has held Sizergh in unbroken succession from the middle of the 13th century and possibly longer. We know from the records that a

Strickland of Sizergh was representing Westmorland in Parliament in 1258, and that the county was in fact represented by a member of the family almost continuously until towards the end of the 17th century.

The manor of Sizergh was bestowed by Henry II upon one Gervase Deincourt (or D'Eyncourt) somewhen between 1170 and 1180, and his family remained in possession for several generations. By 1239, however, the male line had died out. Sir Gervase's great-grand-daughter Elizabeth was sole heiress, and by her marriage in that year to Sir William Strickland the property passed to the family which has retained it ever since.

The Stricklands originated from Great Strickland near Appleby, where they held the manor from whence they derived their name. They seem to have been an off-shoot of the Norman family of de Vaux, sometimes known as de Vallibus, and their name stems from "stirkland," indicating that the lands around their first home were rich in pasture and highly suitable for the rearing of young cattle. "Stirk" is a word still in use in Westmorland as referring to young heifers and bullocks. It is of Norse origin, as is the place-name Sizergh. The ending "ergh" is found in other northern place-names, such as Sedbergh and Mansergh, and signifies a summer grazing or dairy farm. Sizergh, therefore, probably means "the pasture-land of Sigarith," who perhaps settled here after the Viking invasions of the 9th and 10th centuries.

Sizergh is just off the A6 trunk road, about four miles south of Kendal. The road hereabouts is now a dual carriage-way, but provided that you see the signpost in time there is an access opening, if that is the word, between the north-bound and the south-bound tracks. Before setting off to visit Sizergh, however, it is prudent to ensure that you have chosen the right day of the week. In 1950, Mr. and Mrs. Hornyhold-Strickland presented the entire estate, castle and contents to the National Trust. The Trust, in accepting it, agreed that the family should continue to occupy part of the house on condition that, apart from their own private quarters, it should be accessible at certain times to the public. The days and times when the castle is open may possibly vary slightly from one year to another. Latterly it has been open on Wednesdays from April 1st to September 30th, from 2 p.m. to 6 p.m. But I seem to remember a time when Friday was the opening day—hence my suggestion that, to avoid disappointment, the day and times should be verified beforehand.

*   *   *   *

Cumberland and Westmorland, the ancient Kingdom of Strathclyde, were perpetually exposed to ferocious raids from north of the Border, especially during the troubled times of the 14th and 15th centuries, and the necessities of defence led to the construction in both counties of so-called "pele towers" wherein the local inhabitants and their livestock could find refuge when the marauders' approach was signalled. The towers were strongly-built of local stone and were usually two or three storeys high. Into the ground-floor enclosure the cattle were driven, while their owners and others sought safety above. After 1603, when the union of the Crowns of England and Scotland had brought pacification to the Border, the pele towers underwent various changes. Some, of which the one near Arnside is typical, were for one reason or another abandoned and allowed to fall into ruin. Others, such as Kentmere Hall in Westmorland and Blencowe Hall in Cumberland, became semi-ruinous adjuncts to more commodious farmhouses. A third and less numerous group were incorporated in dwelling houses of a later and altogether more ambitious kind. Sizergh comes into this last category.

A short drive leads from the main gates into a courtyard. The castle buildings form three sides of a rectangle, with the main central block, flanked by two double-storey wings of more recent date, facing the visitor as he approaches. The oldest part, the pele tower, is to the right of the entrance porch as you face the principal block and dates, probably, from the middle of the 14th century. It is four storeys high, battlemented, solid, with walls of limestone rubble eight to nine feet in thickness at their base, but diminishing somewhat in solidity as they rise. The stone-mullioned windows at the second and third stages are of later date than the pele tower itself, but the two small top-most windows under an ogee arch are original, of the 14th century.

To the left of the pele tower (from a position still facing the main block) is the Great Hall, built about the middle of the 15th century when it measured some forty feet long and twenty feet in width.

Lady Anne Clifford's Almshouses, Appleby

Appleby Parish church

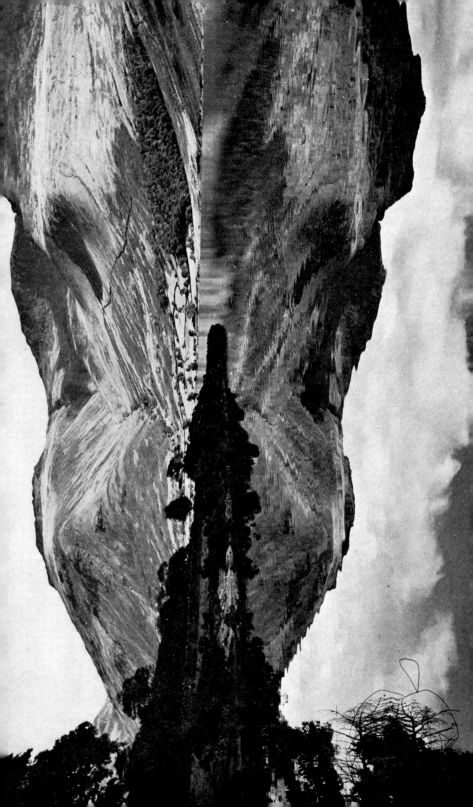

Originally it would have had a roof of open rafters. In the 16th century, doubtless in the interests of warmth and convenience, the Hall was divided and floored over at first storey level, access to the upper floor thus created being by means of an external flight of stone steps. Subsequently the present porch replaced these steps and an indoor staircase was provided. The remaining sectors of the castle are 16th century in origin, with windows of the 18th or 19th centuries. The north-western wing to the visitor's left originally contained the kitchen and its ancillary offices, with bedrooms above. This kitchen continued to function as such until about seventy years ago, but, since by that time the dining room was situated in the pele tower itself, other culinary arrangements perforce had to be made if the family were ever to find the food on their table other than lukewarm.

The right-hand, or south-eastern, wing originally accommodated on its ground floor the joiner's shop, smithy and other such necessary adjuncts to estate maintenance in the self-sufficient days of yesteryear. Above was a long, open-raftered hall, over a hundred feet in length and approached from the pele tower. It had mullioned windows on both sides and a vast stone fireplace on its south wall. Here slept the menservants and other unmarried male estate workers, a circumstance which earned for this wing the 19th century nickname of "The Barracks." Long since past, however, are the days of platoons of in-sleeping male retainers, and part of this long hall now constitutes the Stricklands' private chapel.

Impressive though its exterior undoubtedly is, Sizergh reserves its greatest delight for the visitor who penetrates within. It would be insufferably tedious were anything to be attempted here in the nature of a room-by-room inventory. There is available at the castle a very readable small guide which does just that. It can be purchased by the visitor at the entrance, referred to as he makes his way around this fascinating building, and mulled over at leisure on his return home.

Our purpose here is to perform the necessary introductions to Sizergh and then to hint sufficiently, but no more, at what the visitor may expect to find. His attention will be arrested in the Great Hall (now divided, as explained above, into an Upper and Lower Hall) by the rich oak panelling, the Tudor stone fire-place and the heavy Elizabethan and Jacobean refectory table, chairs and dower-chests,

Wastwater, with Lingmell, Scafell Pike and Scafell in the background

Ravenglass; houses overlooking the Estuary

one of the latter dated and initialled "WS 1571 AS." He will note in the Lower Hall the portrait of Sir Thomas Strickland, K.B., painted in 1600, and also one of Charles Strickland (1734–1800) painted by George Romney, the Kendal sign-writer's apprentice who, born at Dalton-in-Furness, found fame in London, returned to Kendal to spend his closing years* and was finally laid to rest in Dalton parish churchyard.

To the right of the fireplace three stone steps lead, by way of a low doorway, up to the ground floor of what was the original pele-tower, this doorway being its only entrance in those far-off days before the Great Hall was built. The massive walls contain the bolt holes into which the iron draw-bars went home to secure the entrance, and also the stone newel staircase which was the sole means of communication between the various floors of the tower.

Perhaps the most absorbing of all the many fascinating rooms is the one known as the "Queen's Room." It used sometimes to be thought that this room became so called because of its being occupied by Katherine Parr when she visited Sizergh from Kendal Castle on several occasions before her marriage to Henry VIII. This, however, is not the case. The room derives its name from the royal arms richly carved upon the overmantel, with the date 1569 and the inscription *Vivat Regina*. Such loyal sentiments, together with the royal arms, were frequently carved or moulded over fireplaces in the first Elizabeth's reign and later. Indeed, if it is not telling tales out of school, the present writer recollects that in a Midland town which shall be nameless, a certain department store opened a pseudo-Tudor restaurant some years ago. Over the fine stone fire-place was a splendid plaster replica of such an overmantel, with the heraldry picked out richly in colour. Alas, the effect was somewhat marred by the inscription which bodly proclaimed *Vivat Elizabeth Rex* —and this in a mediaeval town boasting a grammar school founded in the 16th century to teach the classics to the more promising youth of the neighbourhood. Could it be, though, that the local craftsman whose skill the overmantel so pleasantly displayed actually had in mind Gloriana's proud boast at Tilbury before the Armada's arrival that, though her body was but that of a feeble woman, her heart was that of a King and of a King of England too? Perhaps.

---

*In a house in Kirkland still standing, upon which may be seen a plaque commemorating his residence.

But to return to Sizergh and its Queen's Room of unimpeachable Latinity. Not only the fireplace and its adornments catch the eye in this fine room. The walls are oak-panelled throughout, and the ceiling is divided by oaken moulded rails into various geometric shapes and figures. Like the other rooms in the castle, the Queen's Room contains several fine portraits and pieces of furniture. There is a Queen Anne walnut secretaire, a walnut mirror of the same period, and three Louis Seize period pieces—a kingwood commode with ormolu mounts, a *bonheur de jour* and a circular table with marble insertion, fluted legs and ormolu feet. There is a portrait, by Sir Peter Lely, of the younger daughter of Sir Thomas Strickland and another, signed simply and mysteriously "J.H.," of her elder sister.

But of greatest historical interest, surely, is that of "the old Chevalier," son of the exiled King James the Second, leading by the hand the youthful Francis Strickland who was Sir Thomas's cousin. Brought up in exile in France and later in Rome, Francis was to become the close friend and companion of Prince Charles Edward, and was one of the "Seven men of Moidart" who accompanied the Prince to Scotland in 1745. He shared in the brief weeks of Jacobite triumph in Scotland, but on the way south, on that brave march which was to end at Derby in divided counsels and retreat, Francis was taken seriously ill and was left behind at Carlisle. He died as the despondent Highlanders re-crossed the Border to the final débâcle at Culloden.

Sizergh is rich in Stewart and Jacobite relics. Sharing their religious allegiance, the Stricklands were deeply attached to the Royal House of Stewart. In many ways Sizergh calls to mind that other ancient stronghold equally devoted to the ill-fated cause of the White Rose—Traquair House, beyond the Border in Peebleshire. Both Sizergh and Traquair are built along three sides of a rectangular courtyard. Each is still lived in by members of a Catholic family which has owned and occupied it for centuries. Each possesses many Stewart reminders, from the tragic Queen of Scots to the last of that royal line.

At Sizergh there are portraits in the panelled dining room of the two last Stewart Kings of Britain, Charles II and his brother James II; of the latter's Queen, Mary of Modena; of their youngest daughter, Princess Louise, and of their only son, James Francis

Edward, "the Old Chevalier." But it is on the top floor of the pele-tower and in a small room leading out of it, that the principal items in the Strickland collection of Stewart relics are to be seen—items too many to be enumerated here but of profound interest to all who find fascination in this colourful epoch of our national history.

*   *   *   *

Less than two miles to the south of Sizergh, where the A590 road leaves the A6 for Ulverston and Barrow, stands Levens Hall, the second of these two historic houses of South Westmorland. It is possible that a predecessor to the present mansion occupied the site as far back as Norman times, though this is not certain. It is known that William de Lancaster, about 1170, issued a charter bestowing upon Norman de Hieland (or Yealand) land at Levens, and this same Norman, who for some reason changed his surname to de Redman, founded a family which was to own Levens for the next four hundred years. About seven miles to the south are the attractive villages of Yealand Redmayne and Yealand Conyers, where Norman may have had his original home. During the 13th century a house at Yealand belonging to the de Redmans was burnt by Scottish marauders. This possibly led to the building of the first important de Redman residence at Levens since it is almost certain that the Hall we see today, like Sizergh Castle, began life as a fortified pele tower. The central portion of the present building is undoubtedly mediaeval and probably represents what remains of that earliest foundation.

The most likely builder of this early pele tower was Matthew de Redman, member of parliament and, in 1300, Commissioner of Array for Westmorland and Lancashire, a post which involved the organization of defensive measures when called for by the activities of Scottish marauders. Richard de Redman, who was also Commissioner of Array for Westmorland and who married a rich Yorkshire widow, Elizabeth Stapleton, enclosed the park in 1393. After military service in the Hundred Years' War and parliamentary service as representative for Westmorland, Sir Richard was knighted and in 1415, the year of Agincourt, became Speaker of the House of Commons.

There were Redmans at Levens until 1580, the last of the line being another Sir Richard who died in 1544. He was the third of

his family to bear the name of Richard and he left a widow, obviously
very much younger than himself, in possession of the Hall and its
lands. This lady re-married, her second husband being Sir John
Preston to whom she bore a son Matthew. Sir John also predeceased
his wife and Matthew sold the property to a Sir Alan Bellingham.
But Lady Preston lived indomitably on at Levens and it was not
until after her death, about the year 1580, that the Bellinghams were
able to take possession of their property.

In the meantime Sir Alan himself had died, and so his son James
became the first Bellingham to reside at Levens. His entry into his
inheritance corresponded with a period of considerable advance in
domestic architecture, construction, interior decoration and general
convenience. He greatly enlarged the house, adding a new dining
room, a drawing room, kitchen and domestic quarters. Hitherto the
kitchen had been a building apart, in order to lessen the likelihood
of fire. Now all was housed under one roof. The walls of many of
the rooms were now panelled or hung with Cordova leather or rich
tapestries, and the ceilings given their plaster-work ornamentation
of intricate geometrical designs. As at Sizergh, Queen Elizabeth's
royal coat of arms was given a place of honour over the great
fireplace in the richly panelled drawing room, flanked by Bellingham
arms and those of collateral kin as though to underline the Hall's
new ownership.

The Bellinghams, formerly of Burneside, were now definitely on
the up-grade and when James journeyed to Durham in 1603 with
other Westmorland notables to welcome King James VI and I to
England, he received a knighthood at the new Sovereign's hands.
In the following reign his son was elevated to the rank of baronet
and, like several of the Redman owners of Levens before him,
represented the county in Parliament. His descendants, however,
were not all of comparable worth and Sir James's great-grandson
dissipated the family resources by gambling. In 1688, little more
than a century after it had been acquired by the Bellinghams, the
whole estate had to be sold.

The new owner was Colonel James Graham (or Grahme), a
soldier of fortune who had served for a time as an officer in the
French army of Louis XIV and later found favour at the Court
of King Charles II, where he fell in love with and married Lady
Dorothy Howard, maid of honour to the Queen. As a result of his

marriage, assisted no doubt by his handsome appearance and his own good qualities, Graham received a number of important appointments. He became Deputy-Lieutenant of Windsor Castle and Forest with an official residence in Bagshot Park. Here he was visited by the diarist John Evelyn, who has left a description of the Colonel's home and surroundings. On the accession of James II Graham was appointed Privy Purse to the King who honoured him with his personal friendship. When James fled to France in 1689 Graham was left in charge of the King's personal affairs. For a time after Dutch William's arrival in England he came under suspicion on the part of the new rulers, and was even incarcerated for a time in the Fleet Prison. When he was finally cleared and released, Graham turned his back on the world of national affairs and retired to Levens. Here he soon became a prominent figure in the life of the county of which, in 1722, he was made Deputy-Lieutenant.

Colonel Graham entertained at Levens on a generous scale, among his visitors being the Non-Juring Bishop Ken, one of the Seven Bishops sent to the Tower of London by James II and later deprived of the bishopric of Bath and Wells because of his conscientious inability to acknowledge William of Orange as *de jure* King. The room occupied by the good bishop on his visits to Levens is still known as "the Bishop's Room."

The Colonel instituted the custom of entertaining at Levens, each twelfth of May, the Mayor and Corporation of Kendal on their way homewards from Milnthorpe Fair. It was sometimes called "the Radish Feast," since the refreshments provided consisted traditionally of radishes and bread and butter washed down with a locally-brewed ale of considerable potency. This was known for some reason as "Morocco," kept twenty-one years before a barrel of it was broached, and on the occasion of the civic visit was supposed to be drunk a glass or tankard at one draught to the toast "Luck to Levens while t'Kent flows."

Levens has four main spheres of interest—the Hall itself, described in a Report of the Royal Commission on Historical Monuments of Westmorland as "perhaps the most interesting 16th century house in the county;" the gardens; the collection of steam engines; and—the legends.

The house is a treasury of beautiful things and of historical interest. Mention has been made of the splendour of oak panelling and moulded ceilings, and these are the setting for a truly remarkable array of fine furniture and paintings, firearms and armour of varying periods, leather-work, tapestries and cabinets full of fascinating objects. And, of course, the harpsichords. One gets the impression of harpsichords everywhere, although in fact there are only two or three. But these exquisite-toned instruments tend to be so rare outside museums that when a house possesses not merely one harpsichord but, as here, harpsichords, the effect is of a multiplicity. The present owner of Levens, Mr. Robin Bagot, is not only a skilled exponent of the instrument, but has one which he made himself in his workshop at Levens and which he has lent to the B.B.C. and to many famous musicians.

Among the other treasures of this richly-dowered house are paintings from the Italian Renaissance to 19th century Constables; furniture from Tudor Renaissance to 19th century Gillow of Lancaster; and cases of documents, including Colonel Graham's commission as commander of twelve companies of the *régiment royal d'infanterie anglaise* signed by Louis XIV and dated 1674. There is a coffee service made in the factory at Sèvres, near Paris, and ordered by Napoleon to be dispatched to his mother. It was amongst other items connected with the defeated Emperor and taken possession of by the Duke of Wellington after Waterloo. There are also a clasp taken from Bonaparte's cloak and a blotter stamped with the Imperial Eagle and a crowned "N", both discovered in the Emperor's coach at Genappes on the day after the battle. The Duke seems to have looked upon these objects as part of the spoils of victory and he gave them to his niece, Lady Mary Bagot, great-great-grandmother of the present owner of Levens.

Also to be seen is the watch which the Duke gave to his A.D.C., Colonel Henry Percy, great-great-uncle of the present owner, who brought the news of Wellington's victory (and also the casualty lists) to London. When the Prince Regent read the names of officers who had been killed he is said to have burst into tears, exclaiming, "All my friends are dead!" The Colonel received the watch when he returned to Paris in order to accompany the Duke on his triumphal entry into the city.

When Colonel Graham came to Levens in 1690 he brought with him Monsieur Beaumont, King James's gardener, who had been trained at Versailles under the famous Le Notre and had found himself without employment after his royal master's abdication. Graham gave the Frenchman a completely free hand with the gardens at Levens and the product of his genius is one of the things which lures visitors in their thousands to Levens today. His plan remains unaltered and the topiary of clipped yew, occupying a quarter of the entire garden, is unparalleled anywhere in Britain, possibly anywhere in the world. To walk on a summer morning along Beaumont's grassy alley-ways, by box-bordered beds of annuals, sweet-smelling herbaceous plants and roses, with the fantastic shapes of the yews as benevolent overlookers, is to step back in spirit into the age of perukes and panniered gowns, of pavane and cotillon, of rumbling coaches in the rutted roadway beyond the walls, and of a peace undisturbed to any great degree by sporadic news from the Low Countries where Marlborough conducted his always victorious campaigns.

The gardens at Levens are not all topiary of course. If box and yew sculptured into curious and improbable symmetries tend to attract the eye and dominate the scene, there are flower beds, rock gardens, herbaceous borders, beech hedges and a noble avenue of sycamores to divert and to delight. And when all has been seen and savoured to the full, there is the Garden Shop where plants and flowers for purchase enable the visitor to carry away a visible and tangible memory of Monsieur Beaumont's miracle. It is nearly three hundred years since Colonel Graham let loose the ex-King's ex-gardener upon his grounds at Levens, and throughout that period only seven head gardeners have had charge of them. This indicates a high record of longevity among Beaumont's successors, several of whom appear to have been Scots. It also no doubt accounts for the continuity of design and purpose which has preserved for this most splendid of Elizabethan houses a garden worthy of its ancient and mellowed dignity.

The remarkable collection of steam engines at Levens is a *pièce de résistance* for the mechanically-minded, as well as for the student of the history of mechanical power. Beautifully housed and exhibited, meticulously cared for, these handsome early 19th century working models are fascinating even to the non-mechanically-minded, among whom the present writer must reluctantly include himself. Powered nowadays, one gathers, from a common automatically-controlled steam boiler, many of these engines were they made to the fullest scale would without question conform to Rupert Brooke's evocation of "the keen unpassioned beauty of a great machine." Beauty many of them undoubtedly have, their technical perfections apart. One small Rotative Beam Engine of the Regency period even has the upper portion of its casing supported by fluted classical pillars crowned with brazen capitals. Confronted with such an engagingly decorative piece of mechanical ingenuity one can almost exclude from thought the dark Satanic mills and the jungles of mean, back-to-back, terraced dwellings created by the same Industrial Revolution which is here personified by these attractive exhibits.

Leaving the engine museum the visitor is liable to be confronted by a mobile machine also reminiscent of a past era. This is *Bertha*, a "Fowler Class" steam traction engine of the kind once used for hauling heavy road waggons, such as those which transported circus and fair-ground equipment from one location to the next. Before the coming of the powerful commercial motor vehicle, these steam giants were familiar sights on the dusty highways of pre-war Britain. *Bertha*, immaculately kept and in full working order, is an impressive and, to many older visitors, a nostalgic addition to the Levens scene.

As to legends, Levens can lay claim to as plentiful and picturesque a fund of these as any house of its size and antiquity. It boasts in the spectral line a grey lady, a pink lady, a white fawn and a black dog—a remarkably colourful if intangible quartette. The grey lady and the white fawn are here mythologically associated. The story is that some two hundred years ago a vagrant woman called at the Hall and asked for food. When this was refused her she called down a curse upon the place, declaring that no male heir should inherit Levens until the river Kent, which runs through the grounds, should cease to flow and a white stag be born in the Park. No male heir did succeed at Levens until 1896 when, on February 20th, Alan Desmond Bagot was born after the river Kent had been frozen over and a white fawn had been found among the deer in the Park.

The grey lady is said to have been seen by members of the Bagot family and others. So has the pink lady, who seems to be a much more shadowy (if the expression may be permitted) figure clad in a pink gown and a white mob cap. She, too, has her supporters, that is to say those who claim to have seen her. The great difference between these two disembodied ladies, apart from the diversity of colours in their costume, is that whereas the former is only to be met with in the grounds—as one would expect in the case of a hardy, outdoor, gypsy type—the pink lady is only likely to be bumped into, as it were, within the house itself. As for the little black dog, he also, it seems, is an indoor animal, with a disconcerting trick of preceding unsuspecting guests upstairs, darting before them into their allotted bedrooms and then disappearing entirely.

Life must be very full at Levens Hall, and for the casual visitor there is certainly much to see and enjoy in this superb period house with its unique gardens and lovely settings. So far as its spectral occupants are concerned, it is at least arguable that many of those who go to Levens expecting a supernatural experience will come away convinced that they have had one. Most, however, will go there to look at things that are lovely and of good report, and they will not leave unrequited.

THOSE WERE THE DAYS

RECENTLY there came into my hands a copy of *The Furness Year Book* for 1905, a private enterprise production printed and published by Messrs. W. Holmes Ltd., of the Otto Printing Works, Ulverston. It is a compendium of the most diverse information, combining a "Dictionary of Recent Local Events" (and some more national ones), a Calendar, a Resumé of the 1904 County Cricket Championship, Dialect Tales, Postal Information, Local Directories, some maps, a variety of photographs and coloured prints (including some from the talented brush of W. G. Collingwood), and very much more besides. All this richness was available to the public annually for the price of one shilling—or by post for one shilling and fourpence—more than 250 pages in all.

Apart from its antiquarian interest, Messrs. Holmes's *Twelfth Annual Year Book* is by way of being a minor social document in itself; a commentary upon the conditions of life familiar to our forebears in the early years of the present century. The advertisements, which are numerous, alone throw a fascinating light upon contemporary products and prices, and many of the photographs illustrate fashions and forms of transport long since out-moded. In other ways things seem to have changed surprisingly little in the course of nearly seventy years. Messrs. Waring and Gillow, for instance, have an advertisement illustrating an upholstered settee ("The Norbury") and wing easy chair ("The Napier), both of which have an almost modern look about them. The settee has "drop ends" and both this and the chair are covered in a tapestry of pleasing pattern. It is only the prices which strike a note of incongruity. The settee costs six pounds, ten shillings and the wing chair two pounds, seventeen and six. Low the wages of those day may have been by present-day standards, but just look what you could get for your money.

No wonder that the "Editorial" to this reminder of Edwardian prosperity tends to be couched in confident, not to say complacent, terms. In "good old Ulverston," say Messrs. Holmes Ltd., "it is a proud thought that business failures are few and far between . . .

Ulverston as a business town is a trump card in the hands of any commercial man who has the confidence of his customers . . ." "Ulverstonians may be slow, but they are sure!" "Ulverston by virtue of its being the capital and seaport of Furness (what did Barrow think of that, one wonders), has resources all its own such as are seldom found in a town of its size."

Splendid stuff. But, alas, even in the midst of such a paean of *amor propria localia* there creeps in a note of stern self-criticism. ". . . we do feel that the state of the roads in and around our district is not to our town's credit. Motorists who visit our charming country all say they are the worst roads they came on." Hard words, even if justified. Already, one feels, the tyranny of the internal combustion engine is beginning to raise its noisy, odoriferous head. Then, disarmingly, there follows a delightful *non sequitur*. "Surely all roads lead to Rome, hence it behoves us to have all the roads leading to Ulverston in perfect condition." As G. K. Chesterton might have written (but did not):

> "God pardon us, 'tis hard on us,
> Our tempers thus to fray,
> Whene'er we drive to Ulverston
> Along the Appian Way."

The pages headed *Annals of our Times*, being a survey of events in Furness—and elsewhere—over the preceding twelve months, take us back to November, 1903, when we learn that, not only was the Drill Hall packed for the "Opening night of the Ulverston Lecture Association" on the 2nd, but also that, two days later, "Addresses were given (where?) by Mr. Chamberlain, Mr. John Morley, Sir Edward Grey and minor speakers on the fiscal question;" while "Two more Armenians (were) fatally shot in London," the murderer then committing suicide.

It would be tempting but impracticable to quote extensively from these "Annals" for the ensuing year. They occupy some thirty pages, and one must be content with a judicious selection. Who could resist quoting for example, under November 11th, 1903, "Teachers under the new Education Act have not received their salaries—'blessings' on the County Council?" Happily, just as one is beginning to harbour apprehensions of militant action by the N.U.T., the "Annals" record under November 17th, "Teachers receive the overdue cheques from the County Council." It may not stir the blood to learn that on November 19th the Annual Meeting of the Religious Tract Society was held, or that on November 22nd the Anniversary of the Ulverston Wesleyan Guild took place. But what cricket-lover can have failed to thrill to the news, on the 23rd, that "Mr. Warner's English Eleven" had defeated New South Wales by an innings and ten runs?" The following day, we read, they were cutting barley in Norfolk with scythes, the Duke of Devonshire was addressing a "Great Meeting of the Free Food League" in London, and a maniac with a revolver had sacrilegiously run amok and caused no small stir within the hallowed precincts of the Bank of England.

December highlights were Mr. R. F. Cavendish, M.P. for North Lonsdale, describing Mr. Chamberlain's fiscal policy as "the road to ruin;" the "English Eleven" winning the first Test Match at Sydney by five wickets; and the Institution of the Reverend T. Edge Wright as Vicar of Pennington, in succession to the Reverend C. Mortlock who had been Vicar for 52 years but was "for many years an absentee." On Christmas Day the Wesleyans of Ulverston provided a free breakfast for 600 poor children, while at Christmas dinner at the Ulverston Workhouse "the decoration of the house surpassed all previous efforts." On Boxing Day they were harvesting oats at Tock How, near Hawkshead, and Mr. Alexander Goodall of Keswick was killed on Scafell.

There are echoes of an Edwardian *cause célèbre* in January (1904) when, under the 26th, we read: "Whitaker Wright, the London financier, sentenced to seven years' penal servitude for fraud, poisons himself before leaving the Law Court, aged 57." In February the Japanese Navy was busily engaged in sinking Russian warships at Port Arthur, the Liberals were winning more bye-elections on the Free Trade v. Protection issue, and "Plum" Warner's England cricketers continued their victorious Australian tour, beating Victoria by 8 wickets and New South Wales by 278 runs. England won the fourth Test (thus making sure of the rubber) on March 3rd, but the fifth and final game was won by Australia, five days later, by 218 runs.

An ominous note appears in the entry for April 9th—"Motor waggon goods traffic commenced in the Lake District." *O dies irae.*

Not even the opening on the 14th of the Lancashire Female Inebriates Reformatory at Langho provokes more sombre reflections. It is a relief to read a happier presage of things to come on the 18th where it is recorded that "Mr. Norman Birkett (is) bracketed top of first-class honours at the Wesleyan Local Preachers' Connexional Examination." Few people in Ulverston in 1904 could have foreseen the heights of legal and political eminence to which that particular young local preacher would one day attain, but there were no doubt many heads shaken in Furness the following day when it was revealed that in his new Budget the Chancellor of the Exchequer had added yet another penny on the Income Tax, now to be an iniquitous one shilling in the pound. Perhaps it was a slight consolation locally when, on the last day of the month and the first day of the cricket season, "Eighteen of the Furness District, thanks mainly to the splendid bowling of A. C. Haines, defeated the (Lancashire) County Eleven by ten wickets and 83 runs."

In June, Mr. J. H. Robinson, the Ulverston to Leece postman, retired on reaching the age limit, having walked 191,690 miles in the course of his 37 years' service. His fellow Post Office workers presented him with a marble clock. It is gratifying to learn, under the same date-line, that "The Alake of Abeokuta, who is on a visit to England, is enjoying himself immensely." Whether King Edward was deriving equal pleasure from his visit to his nephew the Kaiser at Kiel is not recorded, but England's victory in the motor-boat race for the Kaiser's prize would have afforded His Majesty a measure of grim satisfaction—even if, as we are told, "the Gordon-Bennet Cup motor contest at Homburg was won by France, Germany second and third, at 62 miles an hour."

July had its highlights, too. There was an "Earthquake in the North Midlands;" "the Rev. Smyth Piggott, of the 'Abode of Love', Spraxton" announced himself as 'The Lamb of God;' and our editors remark that the Chertsey (Surrey) bye-election, in which the Conservative candidate had a majority of 549 over his Liberal opponent, had been described (by whom?) as the most blackguardly election on the Liberal side ever known in English politics. "No change in parties," they add austerely and with evident satisfaction. The Alake of Abeokuta departed from London on the 8th, sent rejoicing on his way with the gift of a Bible from King Edward "with an inscription in his (the King's) own hand-writing." There was a heatwave on the 9th and "13 persons fell dead in the streets of Paris." The Alake sailed from Liverpool. On the 18th, when the sun heat reached 102 degrees, there is news that Russia has seized and detained "the P. and O. steamer *Malacca* on a charge of contraband of war." "Ructions" adds the Furness Year Book darkly.

On July 19th the King and Queen are reported as laying the foundation stone of "the proposed cathedral" at Liverpool; on the 20th London County beat M.C.C., W. G. Grace scoring 166; the 21st is notable for the fact that "Fifty years today British soldiers were allowed to wear the moustache;" and, on the 22nd, "Russia orders the release of the *Malacca*, will pay compensation, and withdraw her pirate-cruisers from the Red Sea." What a familiar air there is to this last item. Less familiar, fortunately, in Lake Country annals is the mention on July 25th of "a Navvies' drunken riot at Seathwaite Water Works; Vicarage, church and public house damaged; three men shot, one fatally, Owen Cavanagh." As a sequel to this fracas, we find an entry for August 10th—"At Ulverston Police Court, Thomas Dawson, James Greenhow and H. K. Todd, charged with shooting the Seathwaite rioters, were discharged." And, just to remind people that there was a war going on, on that same day we read, "The Russians report the escape of their fleet from Port Arthur; the Japanese land batteries claim to have driven it out." You pays your money. And, as a pair of "silly season" items on August 5th, "A prize-guessing contest has shown a hen to have 8,120 feathers," and "Mr. Coningsby Disraeli proposes a 14 years' time limit for bishoprics."

Came September and a paragraph full of pathos. "It may be wondered," muse our editors sadly, "why so little has been said in *Annals* as to the Russo-Japanese war. The Press censorship has been so severe that of the news filtering through we don't know what to believe, and the war correspondents are coming home, disgusted." In spite of such discouragement, however, they are able to record, three days later, "Capture of Lias-Yang by the Japanese; frightful carnage on both sides."

A more surprising item, perhaps, is that which informs us under September 8th, that "At the Crystal Palace Athletic meeting Dr. W. G. Grace won the 100 yards members' handicap race." As the Doctor at this date was in his fifty-fifth year and weighed close on seventeen stone, the sight must have been an awesome one.

There are numerous references throughout the remainder of the year to the Russo-Japanese War despite the *cri de coeur* quoted above, and invariably each note ends with a reference to the "fearful slaughter" or "frightful carnage." To the minds of most people in 1905, with the blood-baths of Passchendaele and the Somme still more than ten years in the future, casualties of two or three thousand in the course of a single action must have seemed catastrophic indeed.

The County Cricket Championship in 1904 was won by Lancashire, who went through the season unbeaten. This was clearly a cause of considerable satisfaction to the loyal compilers of the *Annals* who note that, "There can be little doubt that this year they were decidedly the best side. The whole eleven fitted into their places and their all-round cricket enabled them to win match after match early in the season." These, of course, were the great days, for Lancashire, of A. C. Maclaren, R. H. Spooner, J. T. Tyldesley and Walter Brearley, with the young Neville Cardus among the worshippers at Old Trafford whenever his fortunes permitted.

The photographs with which the pages of the *Annals* are interspersed carry the reader back into an age which one envies for its freedom from traffic problems if not for its sartorial fashions. A picture of King Street, Ulverston, shows three horse-drawn carts of the "covered waggon" type, only with two wheels instead of four, standing at intervals by the kerb. One horse is being led by a young man in cloth cap, "choker" and shapeless black suit. Two slim young women in tight-waisted, ankle-length skirts, shirt blouses and straw "boaters" walk sedately down the middle of the roadway, while another male citizen in regulation dark clothes and cloth cap stands, also in the roadway, admiringly surveying their progress. The shadows indicate that it is high noon, yet only three other figures are visible throughout the street's length. Another horse and cart photograph is of "Cocklers" with their baskets on the sands at Flookburgh—a tribute to a local industry of long-standing. Yet another horse and trap figure in a "Scene at Booth," competing for interest with a group of small girls in dark serge dresses and white pinafores seen against a background of ancient cottages—a picture truly expressive of the unsophisticated charm and tranquillity of a distant Edwardian summer's day.

But, just as we look back with nostalgia tempered by a certain tolerant amusement upon the people and ways of sixty-seven years

Ennerdale Lake

Thirlmere and Helvellyn

ago, so did these same people of 1904 look back with similar feelings
sixty-seven years to 1837—the year of Queen Victoria's accession
to the throne. Our copy of the *Annals* heads this peep into the year
which gave birth to a new era—the Victorian Age—"How Our
Grandfathers Lived," playing the same kind of game with their
fore-elders as we are here playing with ours.

Under the heading *THE RAILROAD STEAMER, 1837*, the
Annalists quote from their predecessors:

> "The railroad travelling possesses many peculiarities, as well
> as advantages, over the common modes of conveyance. The
> velocity* with which the train moves through the air is very
> refreshing (a reminder that in 1837 carriages were mostly open),
> even in the hottest weather, where the run is for some miles.
> The vibratory, or rather oscillatory, motion communicated to
> the human frame is very different from the swinging and
> jolting motions of the stage-coach, and is productive of more
> salutary effects. It equalises the circulation, promotes digestion,
> tranquillises the nerves (after the open country is gained) and
> often causes sound sleep during the succeeding night, the
> exercise of this kind of travelling being unaccompanied by that
> lassitude, aching and fatigue which, in weakly constitutions,
> prevents the nightly repose. The railroad bids fair to be a
> powerful remedial agent in many ailments to which the metro-
> politan and civic inhabitants are subject."

Had British Rail been able to come up with that kind of sales talk
in the pre-Beeching era, who knows how many of our rural train
services might not have been spared the axe?

The *Annals* compilers have culled many stirring news items from
the files of 1837, ranging from notice of "a sumptuous dinner" due
to be given by the Duke of Wellington to Conservative peers at
Apsley House to an account of a "Gross Outrage upon Her Majesty."
"On November 13th, as the Queen was driving through Birdcage
Walk, St. James's, a man sprang to the side of her carriage and
assailed her in the most opprobrious language, stating that she was
a usurper, and adding, 'I'll have you off your throne before this
day week, and your mother too!' Subsequently apprehended, this

---

*A speed of 30 miles an hour has just been mentioned!

Aira Force

Souther Fell and Wilton Hill Farm

disturber of Her Majesty's peace turned out to be Captain John Goode, late of the 10th Royal Hussars, who laboured under the delusion that he was heir to the throne of England."

There is also a news item from across the Atlantic, where it seems that at New Orleans a "Mr. Alexander Philip Socrates Emilius Caesar Hannibal Marcellus George Washington Treadwell" had recently married a "Miss Carolina Sophia Maria Julianne Wortley Montague Joan-of-Arc Pope, all of that city. The clergyman is suffering from a dislocated jaw." After all that it is almost a relief to read that "In the House of Commons, on December 7th, 1837, Mr. D'Israeli made his maiden speech, which was of considerable length and humour." A pity, one feels, that the Treadwells could not have been in the public gallery of the House to hear it.

To return to 1904. The section devoted to Postal Information makes interesting reading. Some "new Letter and Parcel Post Rates" are set out. "Letters—First 4 ounces 1d; and ½d. for every additional 2 ounces.

Parcel Post	1 lb.	2 lbs.	3 lbs.	4 lbs.	5 lbs.	6 lbs.
	3d.	4d.	5d.	6d.	7d.	8d.

Delivery:　From London and all parts 7 a.m.
　　　　　From all parts 11 a.m. (to callers only).
　　　　　Barrow, Carnforth, Dalton, Liverpool, London, Manchester, North of England and Ireland 3 p.m.
　　　　　Barrow, Dalton, Liverpool, Manchester, Preston and Town Local 5 p.m.
　　　　　On Sundays, Christmas Day and Good Friday there is only one delivery.

POSTAL TELEGRAPH OFFICE. Open on week-days from 8 a.m. to 8 p.m."

What wonderful strides in service and efficiency we have made since those remote, unenlightened days.

Advertisements occupy a considerable portion of the Year Book, and these are revealing in their own individual ways. Mr. H. W. Mackereth the Chemist was clearly convinced that advertising paid. Page after page is taken up with the publicising of his wares. Lamb's British Wines, Budden's Skin Ointment, Doris Hair Cream ("Threepence per Box"), Whitaker's Household Dyes, Meat and Malt Wine ("In Bottles 1/6 and 2/9"), Mackereth's Camomile Pills ("Without

Doubt The Best!") and "Glen Spey" Pure Malt Scotch Whisky, Made entirely from Home Grown Barley, at 3/6 per Bottle— Mackereth sold them all, and much more besides.

Mr. Sidney Brewitt, Tobacconist, of King Street offers Old Monk Mixture ("quite the Grande Chartreuse of Tobacco") at 10½d per 2 ozs., and Flor de Cubeba Cigars ("Unequalled for Flavour & Aroma") at 5 for 1/-.

Thomas Iddon of 10 New Market Street describes himself as a "Merchant Tailor" and "Sole Agent for Dr. Jaeger's Clothing." John Dixon, of the Coach and Horses Inn, Greenodd, refers to his hostelry as "The Oldest Posting Establishment in the District," with "Charabancs, Carriages, etc., on Hire" and "Good and Quiet Horses," a pleasant period touch which is reinforced by a contiguous entry on behalf of C. Wilson and Sons, Carriage Builders of Light-burne Works, pleasingly illustrated by a most elegant brougham.

Many and various are the firms who solicit the Ulverstonian's custom through the Year Book's pages, but none with the prolixity and pertinacity of H. W. Mackereth. Whether it be Rowntree's cocoa, Terry's chocolate, Danson's Eye Salve, Bell and Bieberstedt's High-class seeds, the Erasmus Wilson Hair Wash, Price's Night-lights, Battle's Sheep Dips, or Parrish's Chemical Food, Mackereth supplies them all. The Furness Railway Company has a full-page display of fares betwen Ulverston and numerous stations near and far (London, 3rd class single, 21/3; Manchester, do. 6/5; Birmingham, 12/6;) and where should the Railway Company's Parcels and Enquiry Office prove to be but at Mackereth's, Market Place.

The Furness Railway advertises on another page daily tours of the Lakes throughout the summer—from Fleetwood to Barrow by paddle steamer, thence by train to Windermere (Lakeside), by steamer to Ambleside, coach to Coniston (where tea was taken), then train back to Barrow for the Fleetwood steamer. Leaving Fleetwood at 10.30 a.m., those who patronised this tour were back where they started from by 8.15 p.m. All this for eleven shillings "first class and saloon," or six shillings and ninepence "second class and fore cabin." Should they wish to travel in a little more style or luxury on the steamer, *Lady Margaret*, second class passengers could transfer to first class by paying an extra shilling on board, where they could also purchase picture post-cards of the Lake District at twelve for sixpence.

There are 264 pages in the *Furness Year Book* and all the pages from 244 to 260 are taken up with yet more advertisements of the goods supplied by—guess whom—"Family, Dispensing and Photographic Chemist, Oil Merchant, Bulb Importer, Agricultural and Horticultural Seedsman, Florist and Manure Factor, Tea Importer, Coffee, Tobacco, Wine Merchant and Cigar Importer, Wool Stapler, &c. (rather a nice touch, that &c.) and Agent for and Enquiry Office of the Furness Railway." This is commercial versatility on a scale worthy to be compared, *mutatis mutandis*, only with the mighty names of Harrod, Whiteley and Gordon Selfridge. It is interesting to note in passing that the House of Mackereth's Hours of Business were from 8 a.m. to 7 p.m. at Market Street and King Street, Ulverson, but at their "Ye Old Grange Pharmacie" (*sic*) at Grange-over-Sands they were from 8 a.m. to 8 p.m. Early closing days were Fridays (hours 8 a.m. to 1 p.m.) at Ulverston, and on Thursdays at Grange and Barrow. Grange, however, had no early closing day during the summer months. And just in case these times should prove insufficiently accommodating, addresses are given both in Ulverston and Grange where urgent business may be transacted out of hours. Those were the days—when the customer really counted.

THE GREAT LADY ANNE

THE traveller by road from Penrith to Appleby can scarce fail to see, if only out of the corner of his eye, the pile of ruined masonry which is Brougham Castle. Built on a slight eminence above a bend in the river Eamont, amid lush meadows and flanked by ancestral elms, this venerable relic summons to remembrance whole epochs of North Country history.

Here was the Roman camp they called Brocavum. Here, incorporate in the ruins now carefully tended by the Ministry of Works, is the 12th century keep of the Veteriponts or Viponts, who in Norman times exercised the feudal lordship of their vast domains from its rugged fastness. Their line ended in the reign of Henry III with two girls, one of whom, Isabel, married Roger Clifford, her guardian. So, by marriage, there came into these northern parts a family who were to leave their mark upon it for centuries to come.

The Cliffords were of Norman stock and had their early abode in those regions where Herefordshire marches with the Welsh Border counties. By his marriage with Isabel Vipont, Roger de Clifford became possessed of the barony of Appleby, the hereditary shrievalty of Westmorland and the castles of Brougham, Appleby, Brough and Pendragon. Roger, in fact, did well for himself by wedding his ward, and there is perhaps a certain symbolic significance in the brief inscription, still to be seen, which he caused to be set up over the new gateway at Brougham when he reconstructed the castle, "Thys made Roger"—a statement which can be read in either of two senses.

Roger, however, did not live long to enjoy his good fortune. In 1282 he was drowned when attempting to cross the Menai Straits by means of a bridge of boats. He was succeeded by his son Robert who on the death of his mother in 1291 inherited the Vipont lands in his own right. Recognized as one of the great territorial magnates of the North, Robert was in 1299 appointed Captain-General of the Marches of Scotland and summoned to serve as a Lord of Parliament. Edward I also granted him the Honour of Skipton and its castle. For the next two centuries the Cliffords maintained their tempestuous, powerful sway, from time to time falling foul of their sovereign lord the king and suffering temporary eclipse as a consequence. Several died violent deaths, on the battlefield or on the block.

In the Wars of the Roses, the Cliffords followed the fortunes of the Red Rose of Lancaster and John, the "Black Clifford," gained everlasting notoriety for his brutal murder of young Neville, Duke of Rutland, on the battlefield of Wakefield when he is said to have stabbed the boy to death saying, "As your father slew mine, so will I slay thee." Within a year of this savage deed Clifford himself was dead, slain by a random arrow at the Battle of Towton in 1461. We can imagine the relish with which the victorious Yorkists took their revenge. At an inquest held upon the dead man it was held that he was attainted of high treason, his peerage and his estates declared forfeit. It must have seemed like the end of the house of Clifford.

Black John, however, had left a widow—Margaret, daughter of Lord Vescy—and an infant son, Henry. Margaret lost little time in marrying again, her second husband being Sir Lancelot Threlkeld, head of an ancient Cumberland family whose ancestral home (now a farmhouse) still exists on the outskirts of the village of that name. And now, so tradition has it, to save her Clifford son from the vengeance of his father's enemies Lady Threlkeld sent him to be brought up as one of the family by a shepherd on her new husband's estate, in a cottage on the slopes of Blencathra. Here, until he was thirty years of age, the boy lived a carefree rustic life, unaware of his name and lineage. It was not until the overthrow of the House of York, at Bosworth Field in 1485, that the young man came into his own when Henry VII reversed his family attainder and restored to him his estates. The whole romantic story of "The Shepherd Lord" was immortalised by Wordsworth in *Song at the Feast of Brougham Castle* and in *The White Doe of Rylstone*.

The peasant life and the mountain air of Cumberland had clearly bred one who was no coward or weakling, for Henry Lord Clifford was to fight bravely against the Scots at Flodden in 1513. But the restless, aggressive characteristics of the Cliffords clearly found no place in his make-up. At the coronation of Henry VIII in 1509, he was created a Knight of the Bath and stood high in royal favour. Yet the ways of court life had small attraction for him and he seldom went there. Instead, he preferred the quiet existence of a country landowner, living for most of the time at Barden Tower in Yorkshire and devoting himself to the pursuits of astronomy and astrology. "He was a plain man," wrote his famous descendant, the Lady Anne, a hundred years later, "and lived for the most part a country life, and came seldom to Court or London; but when he was called thither to sit as a Peer of the realm, he behaved himself wisely, and like a good English gentleman."

And with this pious and filial observation we come to the author of it. Lady Anne was born at Skipton Castle on January 30th, 1590. She was daughter and heiress of George, third Earl of Cumberland, raffish and dissolute as a young man, later sailing with Drake to the Spanish Main on a voyage not unconcerned with the acquisition of plunder, commanding a vessel against the Armada in 1588, and ending up as Admiral of the Fleet, Knight of the Garter and Lord Warden of the Marches. All these exploits and titles buttered no parsnips as they say and, since his pleasures and tastes were extravagant, he left his estates and houses in a state of neglect and disrepair. His long-suffering wife, Margaret Russell, was a daughter of the second Earl of Bedford, and she had much to complain of in her husband's treatment of her. Tardily, from his deathbed, he wrote to her asking "from the bottom of my heart, in the presence of God . . . forgiveness for all the wrongs I have done her."

Lady Anne could claim kinship with half the noble families of the kingdom, connected as she was by marriage or descent with the great houses of Percy, Howard, Scrope, Talbot, Sidney, Stanley, Devereux, Wharton, Cecil, Dudley, Lowther, Conyers and Russell— among others. One of her daughters married the Earl of Thanet, another the Earl of Coventry; while she herself was the wife, first of Richard, third Earl of Dorset and secondly of Philip, fourth Earl of Pembroke.

Anne's two brothers died in infancy and upon her father's death his titles and estates passed, by the law of male inheritance, to her uncle and then to his son. It was only upon the death of the latter in 1643, and after strenuous but unavailing efforts on the part of her uncle, her first husband and King James I to persuade her to abdicate her claim, that she finally came into her inheritance. The Earldom of Cumberland became extinct through lack of a male heir with the death of her cousin the fifth earl, but she was still able proudly to proclaim herself "Anne, Countess Dowager of Pembroke, Dorset and Montgomery, Baroness Clifford, Westmorland and Vescie, ladie of the Honour of Skipton in Craven, and High Sheriffesse, by inheritance, of the Countie of Westmorland." It was a formidable citation, worthy to be read out, one feels, against a fanfare of trumpets.

Formidable, too, was the bearer of those proud entitlements, nor did she fail in a proper estimation of her own qualities. At the age of sixty-three she penned some autobiographical details of her early life. After describing, not without evident satisfaction, her youthful physical attractions—"full cheekes and round-faced lyke my Mother, and an exquisite shape of bodie resembling my Father"— she tells us that she possessed "a strong and copious memorie, a sound judgement and a discerning spirrett, and so much of a strong imagination in mee as that many tymes even my Dreames and apprehensions beforehand proved to be true."

She was brought up carefully by her mother and seems to have received from her tutor, Samuel Daniel, a sound literary education in accordance with the habits of the time. Her childhood coincided with the full flowering of the genius of Shakespeare. Marlowe, Ben Jonson and Sir Philip Sidney (into whose family she was later to marry) were of a generation only slightly before her own; the Authorised Version of the Bible was brought out when she was twenty-one, and nine years later, in 1620, she tells us that she "mad a monement for Mr. Spenser the pouett and set it up at Westmester." The vagaries of her spelling, of course, are typical of those of all her educated contemporaries and are not to be adduced against her as evidence of illiteracy.

She was presented at Court (if that is not too anachronistic a way of putting it) when she was only thirteen, and seems to have been received favourably by the great Queen whose long reign was all but at an end. At least she tells us, in her artless way, that she was "much beloved by that Renowned Queene Elizabeth." At nineteen she was married to Richard Sackville, Earl of Dorset, but the union was not a happy one. Like her own father, her husband turned out to be licentious and extravagant, and after a few years of unsatisfactory married life Anne returned north to visit her mother at Brougham Castle.

The journey from Knole in Kent, more than 300 miles over the atrocious roads of those days, would not have been lightly undertaken, even though the Countess travelled in her own coach, drawn by four horses, and attended by twenty-six persons. Her husband accompanied her for part of the way but at Lichfield the pair quarrelled, probably because of Dorset's attempts at persuading his wife to disclaim her rights of inheritance, and the Earl returned to London in a rage. Lady Anne, whose claims were being considered by the Court of Common Pleas then sitting in Westminster Hall, continued on her way northwards. Doubtless she was anxious to take counsel with her mother on the case and on her matrimonial affairs.

She had been permitted to continue her journey with the coach and ten retainers, but before she had been long at Brougham there came a peremptory letter from her husband demanding that coach, horses and men be returned to him immediately. Perhaps the Earl thought that by this device he could prevent the Countess's own return to the capital and thus forestall any further activity on her part in pursuance of her birthright. If so, he had sadly misjudged his wife's character. The Earl's coach and retainers were sent back at once, although the Countess did have second thoughts, sending a messenger after them in the hope of fetching them back. This having failed, she waited until, in the spring of 1616, the roads were once more fit for travelling. Then she borrowed her mother's coach and prepared to return to the fray.

On the second day of April, 1616, the month which was to see the death of William Shakespeare, the Countess set out on her tedious journey southwards. Her mother accompanied her for about a quarter of a mile along the road and there, says Lady Anne's diary, "she and I had a grievous parting." They were never again to meet in this life for on the twenty-fourth day of the following month the Dowager Countess died.

Mother and daugher were deeply attached, and the memory of that last sad leave-taking by the roadside on that April morning so haunted the Lady Anne that, many years later when her legal battles were won and she had entered into her inheritance, she caused to be erected on that spot so poignantly remembered the stone pillar still to be seen standing there today. It is fourteen feet high, octagonal in shape, and is surmounted by a square head. Above this again is a pyramidal cap crowned by a stone finial. On three sides—east, west and south—of the square head are the weather-worn remains of sundials, while on the north side is a coat of arms—those of Clifford impaled Veteripont and Clifford impaled Russell. Beneath this stone escutcheon is carved a "death's head" and the date 1654.

The pillar also bears a lengthy inscription which begins:

"This pillar was erected in anno 1656*, by ye Rt. Honoble Anne, Countess Dowager of Pembrook, and sole heire of ye Rt. Honoble George Earl of Cumberland, etc.: for a memorial of her last parting, in this place, with her good and pious mother, ye Rt. Honoble Margaret, Countess Dowager of Cumberland, ye second of April, 1616."

The latter part of the inscription records the donor's desire that "an annuity of four pounds be distributed to the poor within this parish of Brougham every second day of April for ever, upon the stone table hard by. *Laus Deo*."

The stone table referred to stands, as it has stood for over three centuries, three yards to the east of the pillar and upon this stone, until well within living memory, the pious donor's benefaction was distributed to the poor of Brougham. There is now no village of that name, but the charity is still distributed to needy persons resident with the present parish of Brougham-with-Clifton. The monument, and the bequest which accompanied its erection, speak to us of a great-hearted lady who could be ruthless and determined in defence of her birthright but in the closest of human relationships never failed in dutiful and devoted affection. The Dowager Countess was buried within the church of St. Lawrence, Appleby, and here Lady Anne erected a noble altar tomb surmounted by a full-length effigy of her mother and adorned with heraldic shields.

Lady Anne became a widow for the first time on 28th March, 1624, when her first husband, the Earl of Dorset, died. The two had been reconciled for some time and only two days before the Earl had written affectionately to his wife subscribing himself "your assured loving husband." For six years the Countless lived in widowhood and then, in 1630, she somewhat surprisingly married, as his second wife, Philip Herbert, Earl of Pembroke and Mont-

---

*The discrepancy of two years between the two dates on the pillar may represent the lapse of time between the carving of the escutcheon and the erection of the column *in situ*.

gomery. Although a lover of the arts and a patron of literature, Pembroke was a man of violent disposition. Lady Anne herself admitted that, although handsome in appearance, he was "extremely choleric by nature."

It was not until 1643, when her cousin the fifth Earl of Cumberland died, that Lady Anne succeeded to her Clifford inheritance, with its huge northern estates and the hereditary shrievalty or Westmorland included. For the time being this made little difference to her way of life. The Civil War between King and Parliament had begun and travelling from one end of the country to the other, never at any time easy in those days of deplorable roads, must have become even more difficult and hazardous. There was not, in any case, any great inducement for the Countess to pay a prolonged visit to her properties in the north. Most of the great Clifford residences were in a ruinous or semi-ruinous condition. Brougham seems not to have been lived in regularly since the Dowager Countess's death, though it had received royal visits by King James I in 1617 and by Charles I in 1629. Since then it had remained unoccupied. Appleby Castle had been partly demolished after the "Rising of the North" in 1569. Brough had been accidentally burnt out in 1521, and Pendragon burnt by the Scots twenty years later leaving, it was said, "nothing but the name and a heap of stones." Barden Tower had been allowed to fall into ruin by neglect, and only Skipton Castle, where the fourth earl had lived occasionally and had died, could boast even a few rooms that were remotely habitable. The cost of repair of even one of these derelict houses was clearly going to be great and while the war lasted money for such purposes was not likely to be available.

So for the time being the Countess stayed in the south with her husband, at Wilton, near Salisbury. Given the Earl's temperament, and the fact that whereas his wife was an ardent Royalist he himself favoured the Parliament, the *ménage* cannot have been an easy one. But for the duration of the war, and until after the execution of the King, it survived. Then, on 11th July, 1649, the Lady Anne set out once more for the north.

The journey was perhaps partly an act of defiance. The rebels had murdered her King, and during the past year or so had attacked and dismantled her castles at Appleby and Brougham. She would return and rebuild them, and thus demonstrate to Cromwell and his triumphant Roundheads that despite their military victories they had not won the hearts or broken the spirit of the loyal people of England.

Bidding farewell to her husband, daughters and grandchildren, Lady Anne set off, and after a week's travelling reached Skipton. Here she stayed for ten days, visiting the ruined Barden Tower, and then on to Appleby. In spite of its dilapidated condition, Appleby Castle held a welcome for her. Here she was at home in "the most antient seate of my inheritance, and lay in my owne chamber there, where I used formerly to lye with my deare mother." From Appleby she was able to inspect what was left of Brough and Pendragon Castles, and to re-visit Brougham, "in which Castle and Parck I had not been since the 9th December, 1616." Six months later, on the 23rd January, 1650, news reached her that her husband, the Earl of Pembroke, had died. Once more she was a widow and now, with no conjugal duties to demand a return to the south, she felt free at last to attend to the restoration of her castles.

It was a formidable task to be faced with at the age of sixty, and she must have wondered where best to begin.

In fact, she began where she was—at Appleby. Her diary records the fact. "And in this year, 1651, the 21st of April, I helped lay the foundation stone of the middle wall of the great tower, called Caesar's Tower, to the end it might be repaired again and made habitable, if it pleased God, Isaiah LVIII 12, which tower was wholly finished and covered with lead the latter end of July, 1653."

The passage from Isaiah's prophecy provides an apt quotation in the circumstances and the reference is repeated in the inscriptions on the other restored castles. It runs: "And they that shall be of thee shall build the old waste places; thou shalt raise up the foundations of many generations; and thou shalt be called The repairer of the breach, The restorer of paths to dwell in."

Paths to dwell in were what Lady Anne was aiming at. She liked to journey from one of her castles to another and, as she stayed at each in turn, to feel that by so doing she was not only asserting pride of possession but also demonstrating her sense of stewardship and responsibility.

But there was much to be done first. Brougham, which had been her mother's home and for which undoubtedly she bore a deep affection, had, she tells us, "layen ruinous ever since about August, 1617, when King James lay in it for a time." Skipton, she says, "had layne ruinous ever since December, 1648, and the January followinge when itt was then pulled downe and demolished, almost to the foundations, by the command of the Parliament then sitting at Westminster." Brough Castle must have been in the worst case of all, with the possible exception of Pendragon, for, as the inscription there tells us, "she came to lie in it herself for a little while in September, 1661, after it had lain ruinous without any furniture or any covering ever since the year 1521, when it was burnt by a casual fire." Again the inscription concludes: "ISA. LVIII, Ver. 12. God's name be praised."

It took the Countess ten years to have all her houses rendered secure and habitable, but in the end she achieved her object. The restoration of Brougham was completed in 1652, Barden Tower in 1657, Skipton in 1658, Brough-under-Stainmore in 1659 and Pendragon in 1660. Appleby Castle, as we have seen, was put in order by July, 1653. When we consider how long it can take nowadays to get even the simplest of repair work completed in spite of modern materials, equipment and means of haulage, to have pushed such a restoration programme through in ten years then was an astonishing achievement for a woman who was already sixty when the operations began.

Nor were her castles the Countess's only concern. Many of the churches in the neighbourhood had been badly neglected, and their state was an affront to her devout nature. St. Lawrence's church, Appleby, she found "very ruinous and in danger of falling down." At a personal cost of between £600 and £700 she caused this state of affairs to be remedied and when the repairs were completed she arranged for a vault to be constructed in the north-east corner of the building "for myself to be buried in, if it please God." Skipton parish church, where many of her fore-elders lay buried, she likewise rescued from ruination. Her work here is commemorated, not by the usual mural inscription, but by medallions in three of the windows bearing upon them her initials "A.P." and the date 1655. These windows are of considerable historical interest since they provide examples of that very rare commodity—stained glass of the Commonwealth period.

Nearer home, the Countess turned her attention to Appleby's other ancient church, and to the chapel and parish church at Brougham. St. Michael's, Bongate at Appleby she caused to be pulled down altogether and to be "new built at her charge." Here a stone cartouche on the north wall displays her initials and the date 1659. Brougham chapel she also rebuilt, but little of her work remains, beyond the bare fabric, since the first Lord Brougham, in the 19th century, altered the interior completely. The old parish church of St. Ninian, commonly called Ninekirks, lies across the fields near the river Eamont. This, too, the Countess found in such a state that, as she recorded, "it would in all likelihood have fallen down, it was soe ruinous, if it had not bin repaired by me."

Ninekirks, with its tall canopied box pews, its font dated 1662, an alms box dated a year later and inscribed "Remember the Poor," has survived unscathed from the hand of the "restorer" of more recent times, and presents a most attractive example of a 17th century Lakeland church. It, too, has a cartouche of stone upon its east wall with "A.P. 1660" to remind visitors and worshippers alike of the benefactress who not only preserved it from destruction but also delighted to worship within its ancient walls. It was in 1661, when she was staying at Brougham Castle, that the Countess confided to her diary, "I received the Sacrament there, once at Ninekirks on Easter Day, and in July at Brougham Chapel which I have recently rebuilt." Two years later, possibly in conjunction with the restoration of Pendragon Castle, she "newe repaired the Chapple of Mallerstang after itt had layne ruinous and decayed some 50 or 60 years."

Nor was the Countess's building zeal confined to castles and churches. Her compassionate nature inspired her to provide a hospital, or alms-houses, for twelve poor women of Appleby. Land was purchased, both for a site and for endowment, and in April 1651 the foundation stone was laid. By February 1653 the Hospital of St. Anne, consisting of a chapel and apartments round a quadrangle for a Lady Warden (or "Mother") and twelve "sisters", was ready to receive its first residents. Although modernised in recent years, the Lady Anne's charitable foundation continues to serve the purpose for which she founded it.

All this building, reparation and reconstruction cost the Countess some £160,000. To try to estimate the value of this in terms of modern currency I suppose one would have to multiply it at least ten times. This vast expenditure is all the more remarkable in that not only was Lady Anne the last of the Cliffords but also she had no son to inherit her possessions. Nonetheless, it was clearly a matter of deepest happiness to her that she was able to build up the old wastes and restore to something of their former glory the buildings which were the outward symbol of Clifford power and reputation. It was clearly an immense satisfaction to her that by her efforts she was able to express defiance of the enemies of her Church and King, for when the Lord Protector, enraged at the reports of her activities, sent to tell her that he would pull her castles about her ears as fast as she built them, the Countess replied with vigour that as fast as he pulled them down she would most assuredly rebuild them. Fortunately for both perhaps, the arch-iconoclast contented himself with threatenings. The only sad aspect is that after the Countess's day castles lost their importance and no one thought it worthwhile to maintain what she had so devotedly restored.

In other respects, too, the Countess defied the spirit of the time. During the Commonwealth period, when the Church of England Prayer Book was proscribed by law, when most of her bishops were in exile or prison, and when unepiscopally-ordained ministers had been intruded into so many Anglican parishes in place of their lawfully-appointed but dispossessed incumbents, she insisted upon having the Anglican Liturgy read by episcopally ordained priests in all the chapels and churches over which she had any kind of influence. Once again, while the Government raged and threatened, she ignored their blusterings and went her own ways undisturbed.

Royalist though she was, she could be equally vigorous in defence of her rights after the Restoration, when Oliver's dictatorship and the rule of his major-generals were no more. When Sir Joseph Williamson, King Charles's secretary, attempted to impose a royal nominee as Parliamentary candidate for the borough of Appleby, the Countess would have none of it. "I have been bullied by a usurper and neglected by a court," she is reputed as having said, "but I will not be dictated to by a subject. Your man shan't stand!" Nor did he.

The Countess's journeyings from one of her castles to another, in a coach drawn by four powerful horses and attended by a numerous retinue, must have had almost the appearance of a royal progress. Queen in miniature she undoubtedly was in her own domains, accustomed to giving orders and to having them obeyed. She cherished above all her shrievalty of the county and upon her coffin was inscribed, by her own command, "High Sheriffess by inheritance of ye County of Westmorland." Judging by her burial shroud of lead, in which her remains were found when the vault in which she was buried was opened in 1884, she must have been small of stature, less than five feet in height, but, as is so often the case, her lack of inches was compensated by her force of character.

In contrast to the almost regal circumstance in which she travelled between her castles, the Countess is said to have dressed plainly and eaten sparingly. Bishop Rainbow of Carlisle (1664–84), who preached the panegyric at her funeral, said of her, "The mistris of this family was dieted more sparingly and I believe many times more homely, and clad more coarsely and cheaply than most of the servants in her house." Her piety and her devotion to the Church of England, even in its darkest hours, was exemplified not only in the restoration of its neglected places of worship but also in her own religious practice. She appointed chaplains to serve in the private oratories of each of her houses, and wherever she happened to be staying the day began with the reading of morning prayers and passages of Scripture. She was punctilious in receiving Holy Communion regularly, and always only at the hands of duly ordained and authorised persons.

Yet she could be tough and unyielding whenever she deemed that her prerogatives and privileges were challenged. Possibly the best known and best loved anecdote concerning her is of her dispute with one of her tenants, a Mr. Murgatroyd, a retired clothier from Huddersfield who disputed her demand for the customary feudal payment of a "boon hen." When Murgatroyd persisted in his refusal to pay, the Countess sued him in the courts. She won her case, although it cost her £200 in expenses. She then invited her defeated adversary to dinner and when the cover was removed from the first course there, roasted to a turn, was the fowl over which they had been disputing!

Windermere and the Langdale Pikes

It was a custom of the Countess's to present to every new tenant of her farmhouses or cottages a new lock, stamped with her initials "A.P.", for the front door. But always she had two keys made, one for the tenant and one which she kept herself—presumably as a tangible reminder and symbol of her ownership. The inscription "Preserve Your Rights," which she provided for the column placed in Appleby High Street just below the castle gates, aptly summarises a principle for which she had had to contend strenuously and one which had played a dominant part in her colourful career.

Lady Anne Clifford, Countess Dowager of Pembroke, Dorset and Montgomery, Baroness Clifford, Westmorland and Vescy, Lady of the Honour of Skipton in Craven, and High Sheriffess, by inheritance, of the County of Westmorland, died at Brougham Castle on Tuesday, 22nd March, 1676, in the eighty-seventh year of her life. On April 14th, she was buried in St. Lawrence's church Appleby, in a vault beneath the tomb which she had caused to be made many years earlier. No effigy adorns the sarcophagus, but on the wall above are carved coats of arms displaying the Clifford lineage of which she was so proud.

Lady Anne was the last of the Cliffords, and the castles upon which she expended so much money and effort were destined to suffer fresh neglect and decay. Her lands passed to other ownership; the hereditary status of the High Sheriff's office died with her. Yet this good and noble lady, great in spirit as she was small of stature, lives on in the traditions and memories of her own beloved Westmorland. Like the virtuous woman of the Book of Proverbs, "her own works praise her in the gates."

Packhorse Bridge over Pasture Beck, Hartsop

IN WESTERN LAKELAND

WESTERN Lakeland, because of its relative inaccessibility, is less well known to summer visitors compared with the crowded, more central parts of the area. And not even the grim atomic piles at Windscale and Calder Bridge can rob the pleasant expanse of country between fell and sea of its pastoral seemliness. The little towns and villages—Boot, Ravenglass (with its famous gullery, now under the protection of Cumberland County Council), Drigg, Holmrook, Irton, Santon Bridge, Seascale (haunt of golfers and of family holiday groups attracted by safe sands for swimming and paddling), Gosforth, Beckermet and St. Bees (noted for its ancient priory church and more recent public school)—all blend happily into their gently changing backgrounds of sea, sand dunes, green fields, rolling moorland and, aloofly distant, the tumbled grandeur of the Lakeland fells. Each possesses its own quiet charm, and Gosforth church proudly displays its splendid Cross.

Standing fourteen feet high, Gosforth Cross is yet another reminder of Cumbria's ancient past when, for a time around 1000 A.D., it formed part of that Norse kingdom which also included Iceland and the Isle of Man. The Cross, of which there is a plaster-cast copy in the South Kensington Museum, had a wheel-cross head and is made of red sandstone. The figures carved upon its shaft show the newly-received Christian Faith still in peaceful if incongruous co-existence with the dying pagan mythologies.

On one of the broader faces of the shaft, Loki—the demon of the Norse Eddas—is depicted chained in hell and writhing beneath a venom-dropping serpent. His wife, Sigun, holds the cup which catches the venom and so alleviates some of the demon's suffering. When the cup was full, so the Edda continues, Sigun turned away to empty it and as she did so a drop of the poison fell upon Loki, causing such agony that his violent struggles made the whole earth tremble, and so the earthquake was born.

The cross itself represents the sacred Norse Yggdrasil, the Tree of Life, Christianised, so to speak, by the earliest missionaries to bring the war-loving Vikings under the rule of the Prince of Peace. The Cross, they taught, was the true Tree of Life since because of Christ's sacrificial death upon it, eternal life was thereby secured for all men. Hence, those who set it up in Gosforth churchyard ten centuries or more ago saw no real incongruity in portraying on one facet of it the dying agonies of the pagan demon Loki and on the other the dying agonies of Christ.

Originally there were four such crosses in Gosforth churchyard. One of them was mutilated in the 18th century and its truncated remains, converted into a sundial, somehow survived that period so apparently deficient in any sense of religious continuity. The remnants of a third, known as "The Fishing Stone Cross," are to be seen inside the church, as are two pre-Norman "Hog-back" gravestones and sundry other interesting fragments of carved stone of great antiquity.

Carvings similar to those on the Gosforth Cross are found on crosses of Viking origin in the Isle of Man. There, too, the Norse craftsmen of a by-gone age recorded the twilight of the old pagan gods and heroes—Odin, Freya, Vidar, Heindal and Baldur the Beautiful—as they fight their last suicidal battles and, descending to realms of everlasting darkness, acknowledge the triumph of the all-conquering Christ.*

* * * *

One of the most popular attractions for visitors to the Western Dales or to the Cumbrian coast, of course, is the celebrated Ravenglass and Eskdale narrow-gauge railway. It is only seven miles long but it runs through delightfully varied countryside, with the sea at one end and the highest mountains in Lakeland providing an imposing "back-cloth" of scenery at the other.

Visitors join the train at Ravenglass (the Roman sea-port of Clanoventa, long since silted up), journeying in open coaches drawn by miniature steam locomotives, perfect replicas of some of the

---

*The Anglian cross at Bewcastle, north of Hadrian's Wall, erected in 670 A.D., in memory of King Alcfrith of Northumbria, similarly bears witness to the twilight of the ancient deities, with intricately carved scroll-work, exquisite representations of the Tree of Life, of birds, beasts and flowers, and runic inscriptions which are probably the earliest existing writings in the Anglian dialect, precursor of our modern English language.

legendary main-line giants of pre-Diesel days.* The terminus is at
Dalegarth in Eskdale, where there is one of the finest waterfalls in
Lakeland. There also are the historic and reputedly haunted 15th
century Dalegarth Hall, and the delightful, old-world *Woolpack Inn*
at Boot.

The railway, which in summer months carries something like
100,000 passengers, began its existence in a prosaically utilitarian
way. In 1870 The Whitehaven Mining Company began to exploit
the deposits of haematite recently discovered in the neighbourhood
of Boot. Three years later it was decided that a light railway was
needed to convey the ore to Ravenglass, where it could be trans-
ferred to the Lancaster-Furness main line.

The original track had a three-foot gauge and, in addition to the
ore, some passengers were carried. In 1912 the mines were closed
and the railway was purchased and run privately as a tourist
attraction on a fifteen-inch gauge track. It was also entrusted with
the task of carrying H.M. Mails. After the first World War the
granite quarries were re-opened at Beckfoot, and "La'al Ratty,"
as the line has always been affectionately known locally, was once
more given an industrial role to play, conveying stone to the crushing
plant at Murthwaite. It continued to provide a passenger service
as a side-line.

For thirty years this little railway continued its dual role and
then, in 1953, a crisis occurred in its affairs. The quarry was closed
down and the passenger traffic alone was deemed insufficient to
make it economically viable. It was announced that it would be
sold by auction, as a whole or in sixty separate lots. Great was the
consternation among small-gauge railway enthusiasts, local residents
and holiday-makers alike. A Preservation Society was formed and
an appeal issued for funds wherewith to purchase La'al Ratty and
so save it from extinction.

The appeal was dramatically successful. Money was received
from far and wide, and the Society was enabled to purchase the
line. A Limited Liability Company was formed to run the railway,
new locomotives and rolling-stock were ordered, and since then
the Ravenglass and Eskdale Railway Company has never looked

*"La'al Ratty" now has one or two diesel engines, in addition to the steam locos;
and also covered coaches for use in inclement weather

back. Every summer old friends return and new ones discover La'al Ratty's delights—many of them to become devoted addicts and supporters.

*   *   *   *

Ravenglass is also noted for the fact that in Roman times its harbour, then unsilted, provided a convenient port for the comings and goings of the legions and auxiliaries between Cumbria, the rest of Britain and the Isle of Man. But long before the Romans came and named it Clanoventa, the sandy delta between the estuaries of Mite, Irt and Esk was probably densely "populated." For unknown centuries the sea-birds have bred in their thousands each year on this favoured and now famous spot. Year after year the gulls and terns come back again to lay their eggs and rear their young on these sheltered, bent-clad sand-hills.

Down to the present century the area formed part of the Muncaster estates, and its welfare was looked to by its successive Pennington owners and their game-keepers. Then it came under the protective care of Cumberland County Council, and now it is designated as a Nature Reserve managed by the County Council with the assistance of the Nature Conservancy and the Lake District Naturalists' Trust. The Reserve shelters the largest breeding colony of Blackheaded Gulls in the British Isles with, according to any aerial survey made in 1963, some 8,000 pairs of birds breeding there. The number would no doubt be appreciably higher were it not for the depredations of foxes which take young birds and eggs when opportunity offers. The birds tend to nest in clusters among the tussocks of bentgrass, the black-headed gulls mating and laying first; the terns, of which there are six different species, following suit later. Of these latter the Sandwich Tern is the most numerous, the Roseate Tern the rarest, although the numbers of all six species (the others are the Common, the Black, the Arctic and the Little Tern) tend to fluctuate year by year.

Visitors are welcomed to the Ravenglass Gullery, though they are asked to exercise the greatest care during the breeding season to avoid the nests, with their eggs or young chicks, which can be tragically vulnerable beneath the feet of the unwary. Lakeland offers rich rewards to the bird-lover and student of natural history, and the Gullery and Nature Reserve at Ravenglass provides by no means the least impressive of them.

*   *   *   *

Near the West Cumberland village of Bootle (not to be confused with its somewhat larger namesake in Liverpool) lies the united parish of Whicham and Whitbeck, nestling comfortably under the ponderous bulk of Black Combe. The Whicham Valley, with its ghylls and gullies, owes its formation to glacial activity as the last Ice Age abdicated and relinquished its iron grip on the countryside. It is a peaceful corner, happy to remain aloof from the world's restlessness as represented by road and railway skirting the coast nearby.

The school at Whicham, like many another small village school in past centuries, was once renowned for the notable scholars it sent out into the world. The story is told of a party of "Oxbridge" undergraduates, at the beginning of the 19th century, who called at Whicham's *John Bull Inn* for a meal. When they had finished, thinking to take a rise out of a country bumpkin landlord, they called loudly for their reckoning saying that they would like it in Latin. In a matter of minutes their bill was placed in front of them— in Latin, Greek and Hebrew. The last two languages none of them could read!

Whitbeck church, where according to local lore only the deaf and dumb are buried, is of very ancient foundation. In pre-Reformation times the benefice was in the gift of Conishead Priory, to whom it was presented by Gamel de Pennington, Lord of Muncaster. Smuggling was a major industry hereabouts in Hanoverian times and the church is said to have provided on occasion a highly convenient cache for contraband. Once, when the hallowed building was being used (or misued) in this way, the smugglers had been unable to remove a cargo of spirits by the end of the week. The incumbent was informed of the situation, and the good man (who may well have had a vested interest in the business) obligingly announced that as he was indisposed there would be no service that Sunday!

At Kirksanton, a mile or two to the south of Whitbeck, the mining of iron ore once provided employment for many of the men of the neighbourhood, but production ceased here about the turn of the century. An old legend sought to explain the name of the locality

by telling of a church in ancient times which suddenly sank one
Sunday beneath the peaty surface of an unsuspected tarn, compre-
hensively drowning priest and people. More accurately, the name
derives from the Irish saint Sanctan, in whose honour there was
most likely a cell or chapel nearby. A parish church on the Isle of
Man has a similar dedication, and since to the coasts of Cumberland
came the Viking invaders from the Island in the 9th and 10th
centuries, it is not improbable that they brought with them the name
and fame of this particular Irish saint.

There are remains of stone circles in the vicinity, and at Standing
Stones Farm are to be seen two large upright stones, locally known
as "the Giant's Grave."

*   *   *   *

Muncaster Castle has been the home of the Pennington family
for centuries and is one of the great houses of Cumberland. Originally
a pele tower built as a defence against sea-borne raiders, it was
expanded by the Penningtons in the early part of the 14th century
into a mediaeval castle of a more substantial kind. Then, about
1800, the building underwent yet another transformation, much of
the fortified stronghold being pulled down and replaced by a
mansion house of greater commodiousness and convenience.

Finely sited on the southern slopes of a long ridge, the castle
overlooks the valley of the Esk and towards its surrounding fells.
Green lawns sweep down to noble woodlands, and in spring-time
the immense hedges of azalea and rhododendron flanking the
drives and terraces provide a splendid feast of colour for the many
visitors who find their way there.

But the interior of the castle has items of interest also. There is,
for example, a portrait of Tom Skelton, the Muncaster Fool, who
lived at the castle in the mid-17th century during the Civil War.
There is also the famous "Luck of Muncaster," which dates from
some 200 years earlier. This is a bowl of green glass, enamelled
and gilded and about seven inches in diameter, said to have been
left at the castle by the Lancastrian King Henry VI after his defeat
in 1461 at the battle of Towton. Fleeing from his Yorkist enemies,
he was given shelter by the Pennington of that day,* and in gratitude
left the "Luck" behind him.

---

*Sir John Pennington, who died in 1470.

The legend, or tradition, later grew up that "whyllys the famylie shold kepe hit (i.e. the "Luck") unbrecken, they shold gretely thrif" and also that they should never lack a male heir. The Luck has remained "unbrecken," and while there has not always been a male heir in the direct line to succeed to the property, there have been Pennington descendants at Muncaster down to the present day, and to that extent, therefore, it may be said that the family has continued to "thrif." Besides the "Luck," there is at the Castle a bed which it is claimed was slept in by the King, and also a portrait of the ill-fated Henry holding the Luck in his hands.

When William Wordsworth visited Muncaster in the early 19th century, he found its gates closed against would-be sightseers. The modern tourist is more fortunate, and on payment of a small entrance fee is privileged to enjoy one of the finest views in Lakeland.

At Irton Hall, a few miles to the north, is yet another example of a pele tower which later blossomed into an elegant mansion. Irton also has traditions of a visit from the unhappy King Henry, but it cannot lay claim to the continuity of ownership which distinguishes Muncaster. In the last century it was the home of the Brocklebank family of shipping fame. Since then it has been first an hotel and latterly a home for spastics. As an indication that these pleasant coastal lands to the west of the high fells were areas of settlement in Anglo-Saxon times, Irton churchyard shelters a cross standing ten feet high, with Anglian carved ornamentation and a runic inscription which time and the elements have combined very largely to obscure.

Eskdale is still in the main unspoilt, perhaps because it has no lake to attract the crowds, perhaps because to reach it by car or coach involves for most would-be visitors a considerable detour. Even to travel up the dale by La'al Ratty means getting to Ravenglass first of all. But once the effort has been made, once the railway terminus at Boot has been reached, an uncluttered solitude of woodland, moorland, tumbling becks and mountain splendour awaits the walker and the climber.

Past the little church of St. Catherine the river twists and tumbles beneath overhanging canopies of oak, ash, holly, yew and thorn, its merry water music in spring and early summer forced into competition by the exuberance of bird-song with which the woods resound. Beyond the woods green fields continue until the ancient farmstead known as Butterilket is reached—or Brotherilkeld as it was known to the monks of Furness in the 13th century. After that the walker may make his choice—to the left over Burnmoor to Wastdale, right by way of Harter Fell to the Duddon valley and straight ahead to the great wall of mountain where Hardknott Hause winds up and over past its austerely-sited Roman camp.

*   *   *   *

Hardknott Camp was built in 79 A.D. by the Roman troops of Julius Agricola when he was engaged upon his northward thrust in an attempt to establish complete control of the country. Perched five hundred feet above sea-level on the southwards-facing side of the thirteen-hundred-feet Pass, garrison duty at the camp must have been a tough assignment in winter-time even for Agricola's hardened legionaries. They would have had full need of the bath house, hypocaust and heating system, evidences of which are still to be seen.

Although it lay on a direct route over the mountains between the port of Clanoventa and the important staging-post of Galava (at Ambleside), Hardknott camp would seem to have been abandoned at some time early in the 2nd century. It is possible that by this time the development of a fine system of roads running from south to north had rendered sea-borne lines of communication, with this arduous link route across the fells, no longer necessary. Some authorities have suggested, however, that since finds of a somewhat later date have been unearthed nearby the Romans may have continued for some time to maintain a small rest camp or staging-post here, possibly constructed from the materials of the ruined fort.

The camp site, which is now in the care of the Ministry of Works, was first excavated between 1889 and 1894, when it was revealed that the fort had been about 360 feet square and had been enclosed by a deep ditch. At each of the rounded corners of the surrounding stone walls there was a guard tower, with an entrance at the middle of each of the four sides. A road led from the eastern gate to a levelled-off area assumed to have been a parade ground and for several generations known locally as "the bowling green." Excavations on a site at Eskdale Green, a few miles westwards towards the sea, have revealed evidence of a Roman tile and pottery works. Here no doubt were manufactured the roofing, flooring, hot water pipes and cooking utensils needed for the camp up there on the fell-side. To be seconded in the depths of winter to the comparatively mild conditions at Eskdale Green must have been a posting eagerly hoped for by many a soldier on storm-battered, snow-bound Hardknott.

*   *   *   *

Wastwater, because of its situation, must be one of the least visited of all the English lakes. At the same time it is one of the least affected by the intrusive artefacts of man. Splendid in their austerity, the much-photographed Screes sweep abruptly down to the water on its south-eastern side, while at its north-eastern extremity the dale is ringed around with the formidable flanks of Kirkfell, Great Gable, Lingmell and the Scafells. This is mountain-eers', rock-climbers' country and for a century now the Wastwater Hotel has been the headquarters and shrine of the Fell and Rock Climbing and Alpine Clubs. Great Gable, just under three thousand feet high and offering the climber from Sty Head Pass one of the finest mountain panoramas in Lakeland, was purchased by the Fell and Rock Climbing Club in 1923 and handed over to the National Trust as a memorial to the Club's members who died in the War of 1914–18. Near the cairn on the summit a boulder has affixed to it a bronze tablet bearing the names of those thus commemorated.

In the middle years of the 19th century the landlord of the *Wastwater Hotel* was the celebrated Will Ritson, a jovial character who enjoyed the friendship of Wordsworth, Professor John Wilson of Elleray, Thomas De Quincey and other distinguished men of that time. Many are the stories which have been handed down concerning Ritson, and many were the tales with which he himself regaled those who frequented his hostelry and enjoyed his friend-ship. He had a warm heart, a ready wit and, when the occasion demanded, a caustic tongue. A foolish young man once said to him, "Fancy living here all your life! Why don't you come up to London and see the sights?" "Nay, lad," came the answer, "there's nea need for us to cum up to London to see t' seets; there's plenty o' t' seets cums here to see us!" He could say that today, were he still alive. He died in fact in 1890, at the age of eighty-three, having been landlord of the *Wastwater Hotel* from 1856 to 1879. In his youth a wrestler of more than local fame, his name is perpetuated at Wastdale Head by the waterfall, half-a-mile beyond the hotel, named after him "Ritson Force."

Wastdale Head has never had a population of more than fifty and the church is one of several variously claimed to be "the smallest in England." A certain melancholy attaches to a number of gravestones in the churchyard whose inscriptions record the burial there of climbers killed upon the rocks and fells—a sombre reminder that even Cumbria's comparatively modest heights can, in certain conditions, mean peril to even the most practised and properly-equipped of mountaineers.

North-west of Wastwater Calder Bridge provides the traveller with startling contrasts of an incongruous kind, mediaeval monasticism face to face, as it were, with 20th century nuclear physics. This area once formed the ancient Barony of Copeland and it was a Lord of Copeland* who, in 1134, founded Calder Abbey, the first occupants of which were monks from Furness. Their peaceful tenure was short-lived, however, for only four years after their arrival they were forced to withdraw to Byland in Yorkshire when Scots raiders ravaged the district. More monks were sent from Furness and, in spite of further Scottish onslaughts in subsequent centuries, the monastic life was maintained at Calder until the Dissolution of the Monasteries.

The Abbey then suffered the fate of so many similar foundations, passing into secular possession, to fall into ruin and provide a quarry for later building operations in the locality. From the refectory and dormitory was constructed the dwelling house occupied by the present owners of the property. The ruins of the 12th century church and its later additions are well cared for, their pleasant pastoral setting bestowing upon them that curious charm attaching so frequently to mediaeval ecclesiastical buildings in decay. In these once hallowed precincts may be seen the stone effigies of Sir John le Fleming and Sir Richard his son, 13th century lords of nearby Beckermet, and of two others not now to be identified.

From Calder Bridge the road northwards passes through Beckermet, with its two ancient churches of St. Bridget's and St. John's, on

---

*Most likely Ranulph, or Ralph, de Meschines of Egremont.

through Egremont whose ruined Norman castle gazes disconsolately down from its eminence upon this small town of red sandstone houses. The castle was the home of de Romillys, de Lucys, Multons and Percys, and provided the setting for Wordsworth's poem based on the legend of the *Horn of Egremont* which would only sound when blown by the lips of the castle's rightful owner. Three miles to the west is St. Bees noted for its Priory church, sole remnant of the monastic house founded in the 12th century by William de Meschines; for its ancient Grammar School, the gift of the Elizabethan Archbishop Grindal who was born at nearby Hensingham, and the flourishing public school which has evolved from it; and, as a memory only, for the former theological college founded by Bishop Law of Chester in 1816, which turned out priests for the Anglican Church's northern dioceses until its closure at the end of the last century.

Like Egremont, St. Bees has its legend—one of even greater dubiety and concerned in this case with the origin of the place's name. St. Bega, so the story goes, was a 7th century Irish abbess who landed on the coast of Cumberland with a small band of missionary-minded nuns. When she approached the local thegn with a request for somewhere to establish a convent she was dismissed with the ribald assurance that she could have as much land as was covered by snow on midsummer's day. The good woman bided her time and said her prayers with the result, so the story goes, that on midsummer morning snow fell over a wide enough area to give St. Bega all the ground she needed for her nunnery. Which at least goes to show that Cumbria's meteorological unpredictability is no modern phenomenon and that it is an ill snow-shower that does no good to anyone.

From St. Bees the wise traveller, unless he be of the commercial variety, will wish to journey eastwards, thankful perhaps that his way will involve no closer an acquaintance with the industrial developments of West Cumberland than the village of Cleator, which makes no secret of the fact that it has, or had, close connections with the iron-producing industry. And so he will come to serene and secretive Ennerdale with its lake of ever-changing light and shade, flanked by the long steep slopes of Pillar Mountain (just under 3,000 feet), and consecrated to the interests of angling, forestry, sheep-rearing and energetic fell-walking.

Ennerdale means "the valley of the Ehen," a river which above the lake changes its name to Liza, the English meaning of this Norse word being "bright water." There is little sign of human habitation in Ennerdale, apart from scattered farmsteads and the Youth Hostel at Gillerthwaite. Formerly the *Angler's Arms* was a much-frequented haunt of fishermen and others, but this has now been demolished in the interests of progress or something. Wordsworth used the valley as the setting for his poem *The Brothers*, making use of a certain degree of poetic licence in doing so.

From Ennerdale Scarth Gap leads over into the Buttermere valley, while Black Sail Pass near the head of the dale leads over into Wastwater. This is popular walking country with Pillar Rock, jutting out from its parent Pillar Mountain, providing the expert rock climber with one of his favourite opportunities of risking his neck. At the beginning of the 19th century Pillar Rock was considered unclimbable, but a local shepherd named Atkinson destroyed this belief in 1826 by making his way up the crag's western face. The present-day route was pioneered by a group of Cambridge climbers in 1863 and seven years later the Rock received its final indignity when it was scaled by a female climber. Nowadays, one gathers, to get on to Pillar on a fine Sunday at the height of summer is like queueing for the Centre Court at Wimbledon on a Finals Day.

*   *   *   *

In May, 1810, there appeared in Lower Ennerdale, from no one knew where, a huge, tawny, smooth-coated dog which some said was a cross between a mastiff and a greyhound. Throughout the entire summer this ferocious animal pursued a vicious campaign of sheep-killing, rousing the whole dale in arms against him. Not only had the beast an unparalleled ferocity and lust for blood; he was possessed also of fiendish cunning to a fantastic degree. Never did he attack the same flock on two successive nights. He never appeared by daylight, always picked out the plumpest sheep in the flock as his victim, and evaded with almost contemptuous ease every trap and ambush designed for his downfall.

Night after night, men with guns would patrol the fell-sides, always to discover next day that the killer had struck again—at the one spot they had overlooked or forgotten. Poisoned meat was laid down for him, but he ignored it. A rich sheepmaster offered a reward of ten pounds (worth £100 of today's money) to the men who should kill the brute, but on the only occasion he came within range of a man with a gun the gun misfired! On another occasion a deaf old man was gathering sticks when the "girt dog" dashed between his legs and left him flat on his back, declaring a lion had attacked him!

At last, on September 12th, the animal was cornered in a barley field where a lucky shot despatched him. His dead carcase weighed eight stones. The "girt dog's" hide was later stuffed and exhibited in a museum in Keswick.

SHADOWS OVER THIRLMERE

OF all the English Lakes none possibly, unless it be Wastwater, possesses a more potent atmosphere of impending doom and tragedy than does Thirlmere. Nor is this entirely due to the un-deserved fate which overtook it at the end of last century when it was transformed, at the wave of a water engineer's blue-print from a placid, narrow, river-like mere into a static water-tank of vaguely sinister aspect. Hemmed in on the east by Helvellyn's towering bulk and to the west by the rugged Armboth fells, the lake passes much of its time in shadow, and the sombre note is intensified by the dark conifer plantations which climb the heights on its either side.

The ancient name for Thirlmere was Leatheswater after the Leathes family, who owned and farmed Dalehead on the eastern side of the Lake from the days of the first Queen Elizabeth until towards the close of Victoria's reign, when Manchester money-bags backed by an Act of Parliament dispossessed them.

But Manchester's was not the only, or the worst, crime which cast its shadow over the harmless peace of Leatheswater. A traveller passing through the dale with pockets well filled with cash was set upon, robbed and murdered by an unknown assailant. His battered body was subsequently recovered from the lake. Although no proof was to be had, suspicion fell upon a dalesman of aloof habits and morose disposition. No charge was ever brought against him, but hostile glances and virtual ostracism were eloquent of the unspoken verdict of his neighbours. At length he could stand the strain of the situation no longer. Fleeing from the company of his fellows, he took refuge in a cave high up in the fells. Here he passed the remainder of his days with who knows what sombre thoughts to keep him company.

Out of this grim tale of murder most foul and suspected but unproved guilt one of the most popular of late Victorian novelists, Sir Thomas Hall Caine, wove a best-selling story, *The Shadow of a Crime*. Hall Caine lived in Keswick, and some of the details of his chilling thriller are said to belong really to happenings in Mardale. Be that as it may—Thirlmere or Mardale, Hall Caine or Manchester Corporation—the shadows fell upon Leatheswater in the late Victorian twilight and some may detect their legacy in the trim, urbanised Thirlmere that confronts us today.

*   *   *   *

One of the casualties of Manchester Corporation's activities in connection with Thirlmere was Armboth Hall. It stood upon the western side of Leatheswater, and old prints and photographs show it nestling cosily amid sheltering woods (*not* of conifers), with meadows running down before it to the water's edge.

Here at Armboth Hall, for as long as the Leathes family occupied Dalehead on the opposite side of the narrow mere, lived successive generations of Jacksons, typical in their way of the Cumberland estatesmen of their time. One of the Jackson daughters, however, was untypical enough to marry a Russian, Count Ossalinsky, a man obviously of some substance. In later life the widowed Countess returned to her ancestral acres in time to conduct a spirited rearguard action against the all-conquering forces of Cottonopolis.

The Countess owned four other farms in the area in addition to Armboth Hall, an estate of some 800 acres, and a further 700-odd acres of rough fell grazing. Since her fore-elders had farmed here since Tudor times, the Countess had no mind to see these properties disappear beneath Thirlmere's rising waters. Unless, of course, Manchester made it worth her while. The Countess's rent-roll was just over £500 per annum; the Corporation's agents valued the whole estate at between £20,000 and £25,000. The Countess, on the other hand, set a somewhat higher valuation on her property. Something between £70,000 and £100,000 seemed to her (or her advisers) a more realistic sum. The Land Clauses Act was invoked, the dispute was taken to arbitration (in 1882), and to the surprise of everyone (including, one suspects, of the Countess herself) an award was made which fell little short of £70,000.

After a fruitless appeal in the Queen's Bench Division of the High Court, Manchester persuaded the Countess privately to accept a sum less than the award but still considerably greater

Stone-walling at Underbarrow, near Kendal

than their agent's original valuation. The Leathes family were likewise bought out (at a much less inflated figure), the Corporation became Lords of the Manor of Legburthwaite, the two bridges which then spanned the river-like lake were dismantled, the dam was erected, the waters rose, and Armboth Hall disappeared for ever beneath their newly-municipalised surface.

As for the Countess Ossalinsky, née Jackson, consoled for the loss of her ancestral land and buildings by the generous compensation she had succeeded in extracting from the Manchester City Treasury, she retired to Penrith, to a house in Middlegate, which had once been the town residence of the Musgraves of Eden Hall. In 1890 she gave some land for an extension to be made to Robinson's School. This is one of the oldest in Penrith, having been erected under the will of Penrith-born William Robinson in 1670. It remained in use for precisely three hundred years, being finally closed at the end of 1970.

Castlerigg Stone Circle, Keswick

SOME CUMBRIAN LEGENDS

THE Lake Counties, for centuries cut off by their comparative remoteness from more sophisticated parts of the country, have always provided fertile soil for legend and folk-lore to flourish in. Perhaps, too, an element of superstition in the make-up of the Cumbrian character, with its interwoven strains of a mixed Celtic-Norse-Anglian ancestry, has contributed powerfully to the legendary fecundity of the north-western region.

Books could be written, indeed have been written, dealing exclusively with the legends of the area. Here selectivity must be the watchword, though where there is such profusion selection is not easy. The five stories which I have chosen to form the substance of this chapter are among the best-known of Lakeland's folk-lore and may perhaps be looked upon as both typical and representative.

The Legend of Lyulph's Tower

The Lake-side road from Pooley Bridge to Patterdale is an almost uninterrupted nine miles of scenic joy, with Ullswater offering at every turn some fresh enchantment. But at no point, probably, does the "Queen of the Lakes" (as some claim her to be) show to greater advantage than at Gowbarrow, where the Aira Beck, after its breathtaking descent, finds final anonymity in the deep embrace of the lake. Hereabouts William, Mary and Dorothy Wordsworth saw the famous daffodils which the former, prompted and aided by his women-folk, was to immortalise in possibly the best-known, most frequently quoted of all his verse.

Hereabouts, too, stands Lyulph's Tower, a castellated shooting lodge built towards the end of the 18th century by the eleventh Duke of Norfolk, on the site of an ancient pele tower. The tower is said to derive its name from Lyulph, the 12th century first baron of Greystoke whose lands extended to the lake-side at this point. The Tower is still owned by a member of the Howard family, who have reigned at Greystoke for the past four hundred years.

Not far above the Tower, through parkland which is the property of the National Trust and open to the public, is the famous waterfall known as Aira Force. Here the Aira Beck, which began its career as the merest trickle high up at Dowthwaite Head, plunges dramatically down through an eighty-foot chasm in the rocks. Equally dramatic is the legend which links Lyulph's Tower with the cataract.

This tells how, in far-off times, there dwelt at the Tower (not, of course, the present building) a lady of the house of Greystoke. A lady of great beauty, she bore the somewhat unglamorous name of Emma, and she was betrothed to a young gallant named, rather more romantically, Eglamore. Unready as yet for marriage and sedate domestic happiness, Sir Eglamore rode off in search of adventure and soon gained a reputation for deeds of gallantry and knightly valour, the news of which was borne as far even as the shores of Ullswater.

Meanwhile, the Lady Emma waited with what patience she could muster for her lover's return. But so long did he remain absent that the separation began to prey upon her mind and she developed the unfortunate habit of sleep-walking. And whenever she set off on one of her unconscious nocturnal rambles it was always to the spot near Aira Force where she and Sir Eglamore had pledged their troth.

In due course, the tardy lover, weary no doubt of his wanderings and warrings, decided to return and claim his bride. It was late at night when he reached the Tower and rather than rouse the household he made his way to the beckside, there to rest until daylight broke. It so happened that this was one of the occasions when Lady Emma set out on her sleep-walking excursion to the waterfall. As she walked her footsteps aroused the dozing knight who started up in alarm at what he took to be a phantom. His sudden exclamation woke the lady from her sleep and startled her into making a false step. With a tragic cry, she slipped from the wet rocks into the seething water at the foot of the Force.

As she fell Sir Eglamore recognized her, and forthwith plunged headlong into the stream. With the utmost difficulty he succeeded in bringing his betrothed one to the river bank. He laid her limp and battered form upon the grass, her eyes opened momentarily and then, murmuring her lover's name, she breathed her last.

Sir Eglamore, so the legend ends, overcome with grief, thenceforth became a hermit, spending the residue of his days in sad contemplation by the banks of the Aira Beck.

Wordsworth used this legend as the basis for one of his later poems, *The Somnambulist*, employing, it must be admitted, a certain amount of poetic licence in its composition.

*   *   *   *

The Souther Fell Mystery

Souther Fell, in spite of its name, is the easternmost bastion of the mighty Blencathra (or Saddleback) mountain complex; it is a pleasant, grass-covered fell of no great height, and its entire easterly face is clearly visible to the traveller by road between Troutbeck (Cumberland) and Scales near Threlkeld. Its placid slopes would suggest a scene of no great character or interest. Yet thrice within a decade, in the first half of the 18th century, Souther Fell provided a spectacle which bewildered and alarmed those who saw it.

On Midsummer Eve, in the year 1735, a farm servant declared that he had seen a band of soldiers marching and counter-marching on the side of the fell. Of course, he was heartily ridiculed for his tale, since there were no barracks nearer than Carlisle and Hanoverian soldiers were hardly in the habit of selecting the steep sides of a mountain for the stately, minuet-like manoeuvres of which their drill normally consisted. The story created, no doubt, a certain amount of gossip and amusement, and then was soon forgotten.

But in 1743 a farmer named Wilton, of Wilton Hall (or Wilton Hill, as it is now known) on the valley road which runs beneath the Fell, was out with one of his workers when both saw, to their amazement, high up on the mountain, a man with a dog pursuing some horses, all finally disappearing over a precipice.

Two years later, again on Midsummer's Eve (1745), a large group of people saw an army with wheeled transport crossing the fell at a point where no wheeled vehicle could possibly go. Next morning a number of those who had observed the strange spectacle went up on the fell-side to look for footprints and the tracks of the vehicles. They found none of either.

The only "explanation" that has ever been put forward is that these appearances were some kind of mirage. The facts were fully reported at the time in the *Lonsdale Magazine*, and a correspondent claimed that at the hour when the sight occurred "a Scottish army" was exercising somewhere over the Border. What "Scottish army?", one wonders. Certainly not the Jacobites, since Prince Charles Edward did not raise his standard at Glenfinnan until August 19th of that year. And the major part of the Hanoverian forces were occupied in Flanders, fighting against the French. Perhaps it was Sir John Cope and his warriors, practising for their celebrated stampede from the field of Prestonpans a few weeks later!

Otherwise, the mystery remains a mystery.

*   *   *   *

The Calgarth Skulls

The pastoral beauty of Windermere's shores seems an unlikely setting for a horror story, yet unlikely things tend to happen in the most unexpected places. The lakeside mansion of Calgarth Hall was the residence from 1783 to 1816 of Richard Watson, the absentee Bishop of Llandaff, who erected it at the cost of £20,000, on the site of a much earlier building which probably dated from the 15th or 16th century. Down to the 18th century this older Hall belonged to the Philipson family, and it is in connection with one of them, Myles Philipson, that Calgarth's gruesome legend is told.

It seems that in the neighbourhood of the Hall lived an inoffensive couple, Kraster Cook and his wife Dorothy. The Cooks were yeoman farmers, and were also unlucky enough to own some land which Myles Philipson desired to possess and add to his own estate. The Cooks, however, refused to sell the land which had been in their family's possession for several generations. And so, like Ahab frustrated of Naboth's Vineyard, Philipson plotted to destroy the old couple and seize their property. According to one version of the story (which may, in fact, owe something to the Biblical narrative), he had them charged with some unspecified crime which carried the death penalty and by lavish bribing of corrupt witnesses caused them to be condemned at Kendal. Whereupon Dorothy Cook rose up in Court and cursed Philipson and all his house, warning him that their piece of land should be the costliest that he ever acquired.

So long as Calgarth walls should stand, she and her husband would haunt it night and day until no Philipson was left to claim it.

The old couple were duly put to death—and then the trouble began. Two grinning skulls continually appeared in various parts of Calgarth Hall, a ghoulish reminder of Dorothy's curse. All efforts to destroy the skulls proved useless. They were burned by fire; they were crushed to fine dust; they were cast into the lake. But still they returned, relentless reminders of Myles Philipson's crime.

At last, as Dorothy had prophesied, the Philipson line no longer held Calgarth, and forthwith the curse ceased to operate. The skulls were seen no more. Calgarth Hall is now a children's orthopaedic hospital, and whatever grim deeds may once have darkened its fame have long since been outweighed by deeds of mercy and compassion.

*   *   *   *

The "Luck" of Eden Hall

Eden Hall, near Penrith, was for centuries the home of the ancient family of Musgrave. It was totally demolished during the period between the two world wars. It is still remembered, however, on account of the famous "Luck" so long connected with the mansion. This is an ancient glass vessel, green in colour, decorated with enamels of red, yellow and blue. It is shaped like a beaker, narrow at the base but widening to a broad lip at the top. It is contained in a leather case, adorned with vine leaves and with the sacred monogram IHS stamped upon the lid.

Various theories as to its origin have been propounded. Some antiquaries have declared its decorations to be Saracenic in design, and have suggested that it might have been brought from Palestine by some early Crusading Musgrave. Others have declared it to be a glass chalice, brought into use when Communion vessels of precious metal were too costly, or too vulnerable, in view of the predatory habits of Scots raiders from across the Border. This may be so, but it seems doubtful, since pewter was so frequently used for altar vessels when gold or silver could not be afforded.

Of course the most romantic account of the Luck's origin is the most popular—and the least probable. According to this legend a servant from Eden Hall went out one summer's night to fetch

water from the so-called Fairy Well. In a grassy hollow near the
well, he came suddenly upon a band of fairies dancing in a ring
around an object which proved, on closer inspection, to be a glass
goblet. Attracted by its unusual design and rich adornments, the
servant strode into the fairy circle and seized the goblet. Thereupon
the fairies began to chant in chorus:

> "If this cup should break or fall,
> Farewell the luck of Eden Hall."

It is said that whenever the Luck was brought out by the Musgraves
to show to their visitors the greatest care was taken to see that no
harm befell it. Now Eden Hall has gone and the Luck, so rumour
has it, reposes in safety beyond compare—in the strong vaults of
the Bank of England.

*   *   *   *

King Dunmail's Grave

The traveller crossing Dunmail Raise* on his way northwards
from Grasmere to Keswick will almost certainly notice at the
summit a great cairn of rough stones. This, he will be told, covers
the grave of King Dunmail. The cairn has certainly stood there for
a very long time.

In the tenth century A.D. what is now Cumberland still formed
part of the British (i.e., Celtic) kingdom of Strathclyde, which
included also the south-western parts of the Scottish Lowlands.
Dunmail (otherwise known as Dumnail or Durenald) was the last
of its native rulers. In 945, the Saxons under King Edmund invaded
Cumbria, and at a great battle traditionally fought on the Raise
itself decisively defeated Dunmail and so brought the Celtic
Kingdom to an end.

So much for the history; what about the legend? According to
this, Dunmail was slain in the fighting and was buried by his hench-
men at the summit of the Raise. Over his grave the defeated Britons
were said to have built the cairn, more stones being added year by
year.

But the legend does not end there. As he lay a-dying, Dunmail
is said to have told his most devoted warriors that one day he would

---

*The Norse word *hreysi* indicates a road across the mountains.

return and lead them once more against the Saxon invaders. Then, just as the dying King Arthur is said to have bidden Sir Bedivere to take his sword *Excalibur* and fling it into the mere, so Dunmail bade his followers take the golden circlet from his helmet and hide it where the foe could never find it.

So the faithful warriors took the bright crown and, after they had buried their fallen king, climbed the steep sides of Helvellyn and cast it into Grisedale Tarn. Then they vanished into the enshrouding mists, to await the summons to go forth once more to battle. And once a year, so the legend continues, they raise the circlet from the still waters of the tarn and carry it to the cairn where their king lies buried. There they strike the stones three times with their spears to inform the sleeping Dunmail that they are ready. But always comes the royal reply—"Not yet, my warriors; wait a while yet." And once again the phantom army vanishes into the mist as it comes swirling down the silent fellside.

It is a romantic story, rich with the atmosphere of Arthurian myth and of the mysterious Celtic twilight. It is sad to think that the reality should be so prosaic by contrast. King Dunmail is known to have died in Rome some thirty years after his defeat by Edmund. And, alas, the cairn, past which the motorised traffic thunders in summer in an almost unceasing stream, is probably nothing more than an ancient county boundary mark, standing as it does almost on the demarcation line dividing Cumberland and Westmorland.

When Thirlmere was being converted into a reservoir by Manchester Corporation towards the end of last century, it was decided to give the cairn a general tidy-up, more in keeping with the traditions of a great city. A start was being made with this well-meaning project when word of it reached the ears of Canon Rawnsley in Keswick, ever prepared to up and do battle with the Philistines. Terrible the wrath, one imagines, of this redoubtable defender of traditional Lakeland at this latest example of urban insensitivity, with the telephone cables to Manchester fairly sizzling with the ardour of his protests. At all events, the great man and the National Trust he had helped to found were not to be taken lightly. Counter orders were hastily forthcoming from Cottonopolis, and King Dunmail's cenotaph was left unmolested in all its picturesque decrepitude.

WINDERMERE YESTERDAYS

WINDERMERE, "England's greatest standing water," is inevitably the most "popular" of the English Lakes, in the most pejorative sense of the word "popular." This is partly because of its length, nearly eleven miles from Waterhead in the north to Newby Bridge in the south; and partly because it is the most southerly and therefore the most accessible—particularly so, of course, since the opening in 1970 of the northern sections of the M6 motorway.

Because of its length Windermere lends itself, in a way that none of the lesser lakes does, to mechanised aquatic diversions such as speed-boat racing and water-skiing. Because of its accessibility, Bowness Bay and Waterhead (Ambleside) tend to take on in high season rather too much of the atmosphere of Blackpool or Douglas. Because of a combination of these two characteristics of spaciousness and proximity to the heavily-populated areas of the North, the lake affords anchorage and "sea-room" for an ever-multiplying number of power-driven craft of various kinds. Inevitable, no doubt, but regrettable to those who come to the Lakes in search of quiet relaxation and unspoilt natural beauty. Such people undoubtedly do well to avoid in high summer the places I have mentioned. But in late autumn, winter or early spring the lake recovers a good deal of its ancient peace, and has delights to offer that the summer crowds know not of.

On a calm October day the surface of the water, once the mists of early morning have dispersed, assumes a mirror-like quality, reflecting uncannily the still unfallen foliage of the woods which fringe so much of Windermere's shores and cover most of her islands. Later in the month and throughout the early days of November, that same foliage is transformed as it changes from green to yellow, orange, bronze, russet or deepest crimson hue. And then, as the first frosts and gales of winter make themselves felt, the leafage disappears to reveal "bare, ruined choirs" of columned trunks, topped by the delicate tracery of branch and twig. After Christmas, when there is snow on the fells and the trees are adorned with a fairyland filigree of silver frosting, Windermere is again transformed —this time into a sparkling wonderland designed, one might almost think, for some "super-colossal" pantomimic spectacle on ice.

But it is when the hounds of spring have at last broken loose from winter's traces that the supreme loveliness of Lakeland is to be seen—on and around Windermere as elsewhere. Then the sharp blue of the sky is reflected in the sparkling waters as the stiff easterly breeze ruffles the still unfrequented surface of the water and the fleecy whiteness of the speeding clouds is matched in the fields by the woolly antics of the black-faced lambs. In turn, primrose, crocus, daffodil, violet, bluebell and buttercup gladden the eye and cheer the spirit—until such time as their modest glories give place to the showier splendours of the azaleas and rhododendrons which lend to the gardens of Bowness, Ambleside, Clappersgate and the large houses all round the lake so brave and flamboyant a May-time flowering. No; Windermere is not all iced-lollies and litter and milling crowds. But you need to choose your time to visit her if you wish to see her at her undistracted best.

Three-quarters of Windermere's shore is in Lancashire; the remaining quarter—from Storrs to Waterhead—is in Westmorland. If the Lake is approached from the south—from Ulverston, Barrow or Cartmel—contact is made at Newby Bridge. Here is the outflow of the lake, continuing as the river Leven by way of Backbarrow to the sea at Greenodd.

Newby Bridge itself retains its ancient straitness, with embrasures for pedestrian refuge on the parapet on either side. I suppose that any time now some insensitive, interfering bureaucrat will decide that it must be replaced by a four-lane concrete hideosity "in the interests of modern traffic," and the internal combustion engine will have won yet another victory over what is sane and seemly and part of our national inheritance. Meanwhile it is still there, where it has stood for centuries, to delight the eye of all whose standards of value remain unwarped by the machine with its perennial and insatiable requirements.

At the northern end of the Bridge stands the *Swan Hotel*, an ancient hostelry whose oldest proportions strike the eye more pleasingly than do some of its more recent additions. Internally, the main part of the hotel remains unspoilt and unsmartened up, and more than one excellent afternoon tea have I enjoyed seated before a log fire in one of its comfortable and commodious armchairs. How pleasant it is when one finds an ancient hostelry whose simple dignities have been suffered to remain, where no attempt has been made to "jazz up" its homely decencies in the supposed interests of the "gin-and-Jag" set. Who wants to see an honest Cumbrian inn of white-washed stone walls, green slate roof, blue-flagged floor and old oak beams tricked out in tubular furnishings, chrome fittings, neon lighting and an ostentatious array of bottles containing spirituous and wildly expensive liquors? Who wants to drop into an inn after a day on the fells to be confronted with an over-sized menu card, half of it in Soho French, offering one a lot of pretentious-sounding snob food at grossly inflated prices when one would gladly settle for a bowl of Scotch broth and a well-cooked shepherd's pie? There *are* still country inns which serve simple, wholesome fare at reasonable prices, but they become harder to find every year.

Beyond Newby Bridge on the western side of the lake the road winds through woods to Lakeside. Here are the piers from which the Windermere "steamers" (actually they are propelled by diesel-driven engines) ply up the lake to Bowness and Ambleside. Here, too, in days gone by, was the terminus of the branch railway line from Ulverston. Excursion trains from Barrow and much further afield brought day trippers to crowd the decks of the steamers, until nationalisation and the motor car combined to render this attractive little line uneconomic. It was closed down some years ago and its rails removed. Now a group of "steam" enthusiasts has purchased a section of the old line, and steam-hauled trains carry passengers once more from Haverthwaite to Lakeside as a summer-time, private enterprise.

There is surely no pleasanter or more satisfactory way of seeing Windermere than from the deck of one of British Rail's aptly-named vessels—*Teal*, *Tern* and *Swan*. In winter these craft are laid up for overhaul. They run for a week or two at Easter and then rest at their moorings until just before Whitsun. It was on the first day of their summer season proper that a party of fifty of us went aboard one of them for a trip to Waterhead. It was a perfect May day—cloudless, sunny, but not too hot. The gentle breeze did little more than ruffle the surface of the water. So early in the season we virtually had the craft to ourselves. Had we chartered it specially and ordered the weather, things could not have turned out more agreeably for

144   LAKE COUNTRY ECHOES

us. As our vessel pursued its placid course between the low wooded hills on either shore and the equally wooded islands, the central Lakeland fells loomed up ahead of us, dramatically increasing in bulk as we approached them. Over beyond our port bow to the north-west the Langdale Pikes reared their unmistakably characteristic shapes.

At the narrowest point of the lake our route cut at right angles across that of the Ferry which carries cars and pedestrians (mostly cars nowadays) shuttling from one side to the other during the daylight hours. A century or more ago there were three ferries in constant use; now there is only one. A ferry at the upper end of the lake crossed from Miller Ground to somewhere near where Wray Castle now stands, while another crossed the southern end of the lake in the Lakeside–Stott Park area. The still existing central route is easily the most ancient, in mediaeval times providing not only a direct passage for farmers and wool merchants between the flourishing markets at Hawkshead and Kendal, but also for the more pious purposes of pilgrims visiting the chantry chapel on St. Mary's Holm with its resident staff of Scottish priests.

Mention of this important link between the Lancashire and Westmorland shores of Windermere would be incomplete without some reference to the disaster which befell the Ferry on the evening of October 19th, 1635. The ferry boat, presumably propelled by sail or oars or a combination of both, was boarded by a party of forty-seven people returning to Kendal from a wedding at Hawkshead. With them they had a number of carriages and eleven horses. It sounds an alarmingly heavy load, particularly when it is remembered that the modern power-driven ferry boat is well loaded with eight or so cars on board. Yet, all would probably have been well had the lake remained reasonably calm. When they were about half-way across, however, a sudden fierce squall seems to have sprung up, the craft was swamped and capsized, and all her passengers were drowned.

There was for many generations an inn on the Lancashire side of the Ferry, somewhere near the foot of the brow, but all trace of it has now disappeared. The imposing building near the present Ferry landing was built as an hotel during the last century, and continued as such until the outbreak of War in 1939. Now it houses the offices and laboratories of the Freshwater Biological Research Association.

Towering over Lakeside steamer jetty, at the southern end of Windermere, is the tree-covered Finsthwaite Fell, notable for the tower which crowns its summit. This was built in 1799 to celebrate the naval victories of Camperdown, Cape St. Vincent and the Nile. It bears an inscription eulogising "the officers, seamen and marines of the Royal Navy, whose matchless conduct and irresistible valour decisively defeated the fleets of France, Spain and Holland, and promoted and protected liberty and commerce."

But Finsthwaite has another item of interest for the visitor who is a snapper-up of curious and unconsidered trifles, and who succeeds in finding his way to its tree-protected churchyard. This is the grave of Princess Clementine Johannes Sobieska Douglas, who came to live at Waterside House in 1745 and who died there in 1771. She was a great recluse, and consequently the subject of much speculation in the neighbourhood. One local tradition described her as a lady with wonderfully fair hair. Another claimed her to be the daughter of Prince Charles Edward—a manifest absurdity, as can be seen by a brief comparison of dates. The Prince was only 25 in 1745 when the Princess is said to have taken up residence at Waterside House!

It is easy to see how the confusion arose. Prince Charles Edward's mother was Princess Maria Clementina Sobieska, grand-daughter of King John Sobieski of Poland. It is possible that the "Finsthwaite Princess" was a relation, possibly even a cousin, of "Bonnie Prince Charlie" and perhaps the widow of some obscure Scottish soldier of fortune, of whom there were many in foreign service after the failure of the Rising of 1715. One hopes that the lady, whoever she was, found peace in her Waterside seclusion.

Storrs Hall, about half-way along the eastern shore of Windermere, is an italianate mansion (now an hotel), built in the 18th century, but purchased and enlarged in 1807 by John Bolton, a Liverpool merchant of great wealth—mostly made in the West Indian rum and sugar trades. Here, in the year 1825, the hospitable Mr. Bolton had as his guests George Canning (Foreign Secretary and future Prime Minister), Sir Walter Scott and J. G. Lockhart, the latter being Scott's son-in-law and biographer. The entertainment began with a dinner party, at which Wordsworth, Southey and John Wilson of Elleray ("Christopher North") were also guests. The final day of the visit of Scott and Canning, August 25th, was the day of the great "regatta." As self-appointed "Admiral of the Lake," Professor Wilson seems to have been in charge of the proceedings. These consisted, not of races, but of a prolonged procession of gaily-decorated barges weaving its way in and out of the bays and islands. It was a gloriously sunny day, the shores of the lake were plentifully peopled with excited spectators, and everyone was happy.

The climactic moment came when the flotilla arrived off Storrs Hall. Here it hove to, to admit into what Lockhart calls "the place of honour" (the head of the column?) the vessel bearing Mr. Bolton and his three illustrious guests. They were greeted with loud cheers from the other boats, led by Wordsworth, Wilson and Southey, that trio of Lakelanders as distinguished in their own right as the two notable Scots and the great statesman they had come to honour.

*   *   *   *

One of the oddest and most unliterary of the Lake "poets" was surely the strange 19th century character known as "Poet Close." He was born in Swaledale, Yorkshire, in 1816, the son of a butcher, and early in life settled in Kirkby Stephen where he established himself as a printer. Here he also started to write his verses, which he printed himself and issued in booklet form.

Every summer he used to set up a bookstall at Bowness-on-Windermere and try to beguile passing holiday-makers into buying his wares. Those who did so were treated to a flow of most fulsome praise; those who did not, to torrents of violent abuse. Alas! those who did not buy were invariably more than those who did, for poor Close's verses were doggerel of the direst kind. Although he held the most exalted opinion of his own poetic powers, he was in fact a sort of Cumbrian McGonnigal. Those who failed to appreciate his genius he dismissed contemptuously and abusively as fools and knaves.

Nevertheless, his sheer persistence in producing and publicising his verses, together with his assiduity in flattering the local nobility and gentry in verse, earned him a dubious kind of notoriety. It also gained for him, through the efforts of some of the more gullible of his influential patrons, a Civil List pension of £50 a year. *Punch* ridiculed the award and questions were asked in the House of Commons. Ultimately the pension was withdrawn and Close was granted £100 by way of compensation. He died at Kirkby Stephen in 1891.

*   *   *   *

Windermere is dotted with a number of small islands which add greatly to its attractions. All of them are well covered with trees; many in spring-time are profuse in lily-of-the-valley and other wild flowers. The chantry on St. Mary's Holm, or Lady Holm, mentioned above, was founded by the de Lindesay family in 1256. It shared the fate of all such shrines under Henry VIII, but as late as Wordsworth's time there were still traces of it to be seen, and reference to it is contained in *The Prelude*.

The largest of the islands also has connections with the de Lindesays, a family of Norman-Scottish extraction. It was the home of Walter de Lindesay, who had been formerly Scottish ambassador to the Court of King Henry III and died on the island in 1272. Later the island, then known simply as The Holm, passed into the hands of the Philipsons of Calgarth. Eventually it came into the possession of the Curwens of Workington Hall when, in 1790, Isabel Curwen bought it for £14,000. In that year Isabel married her cousin John Christian, who not only took the name of Curwen as his own but also re-named the island Belle Isle in honour of his wife. Belle Isle remained in the possession of the Curwen family until recent times, when it finally became the property of the National Trust.

Calgarth Hall, once the home of the Philipsons, was occupied in Wordsworth's time by Bishop Watson of Llandaff, in many respects a typical 18th century prelate who saw nothing reprehensible about living in Westmorland while drawing the emoluments from a South Wales bishopric. The son of a Headmaster of Heversham Grammar School, Watson was a good mathematician who did well at Cambridge. When the Chair of Chemistry in that University fell vacant, although he knew next to nothing of the subject he somehow bluffed his way into being nominated for it, catching up on the subject, so to speak, after he had been appointed to teach it. When the Professorship of Divinity later fell vacant he employed a similar technique, in this case diverting one third of the stipend to the payment of a substitute lecturer. When he was given the bishopric of Llandaff, Watson married, bought Calgarth and settled down to a comfortable country house existence on the shores of Windermere.

There is some dispute as to the frequency with which he visited his distant diocese but the most charitable accounts credit him with having made the journey at least once every three years. Theoretically he was opposed to absenteeism and issued on one occasion a strongly-worded warning to his clergy about the evils of non-residence. De Quincey, who knew him well, considered him personally pompous and uninteresting, but found the Bishop's deep preoccupation with his material prospects and hope of further advancement entirely fascinating. Wordsworth's opinion of the Bishop was scarcely more exalted. Watson was an indefatigable planter of trees, but he enraged the poet by planting principally quick-growing (and therefore profitable) but non-indigenous larches. On the rare occasions when Bishop Watson journeyed to London and took his seat in the House of Lords, he invariably supported the Whig Governments of the time. It was with a profound sense of grievance, therefore, that for the vacant Archbishopric of York he discovered that he had been passed over for another and doubtless less deserving man. Conceivably the churchpeople of Llandaff shared his dismay.

*   *   *   *

At the beginning of the 19th century there was no village of Windermere—only a cluster of cottages at what was then known as Birthwaite—"the clearing among the birch trees"—near where the station now stands. It was only when the railway came in 1847, and numerous houses sprang up around it, that the area took unto itself the name of the lake a mile distant.

Bowness, too, was then but a group of small houses and two inns gathered in companionable irregularity about the mediaeval church of St. Martin, most of which dates from the 15th century although there was a church on the site long before that. St. Martin's possesses some magnificent ancient stained glass, particularly in the east window. Much of this glass dates from the 14th century and was originally in Cartmel Priory Church. It is believed to have been brought to Bowness to preserve it from destruction at the time the Priory was dissolved. There are some chained books, dating from the 16th century, to be seen in a case in the church, and a carving of a century or so later showing the church's patron saint, St. Martin,

Matterdale church

sharing his military cloak with the beggar of the legend. American visitors like to discover the arms of the Washington family in one of the lights of the east window.

There are some curious territorial features about Windermere. We have already seen that all the western shore and the southern half of the eastern shore are in Lancashire, while the northern half of the eastern shore is in Westmorland. But the *bed* of the lake is entirely in Westmorland. This is because it once appertained to the ancient Barony of Kendal, the rights of which have descended by devious means to the present Earl of Lonsdale. Ecclesiastically the whole lake is in the parish of Windermere (St. Martin's), and at one time the Vicar of that church was entitled to maintain a boat on the lake free of all charges and also to a tithe of all fish caught therein. This is a survival into the post-Reformation era of the grant made to Furness Abbey in the 13th century by William de Lancaster, Baron of Kendal, of the right to maintain a boat and twenty nets on the late, as well as a raft for the transportation of timber. The right to net the famous Windermere char, that "golden Alpine trout" as Camden called it, must have been highly prized by the monks, especially on the many days of abstinence when flesh meat was prohibited.

To the north of the Ferry, on the western or Lancashire side of the lake, the National Trust has acquired a large area of thickly-wooded land on the slopes of the Claife Heights. Although there is no access for cars beyond a certain point, clearly signposted pathways provide, amid unspoilt surroundings, for the needs of ramblers and nature lovers. The walker who starts at the Ferry and follows this trail emerges at High Wray where, in 1875, the celebrated Hardwicke Drummond Rawnsley, later to become one of the co-founders of the National Trust, was appointed Vicar. When, a year later, he married Edith Fletcher of The Croft, Clappersgate, Wray Vicarage became the centre of a lively group of intellectuals who foregathered there during the Long Vacations. Among this band were such men as J. M. Shorthouse, author of *John Inglesant*, Edward Thring, the famous reforming Headmaster of Uppingham, and many others.

Wray Castle, at Low Wray, is an entirely spurious "mediaeval" fortress, all sham turrets, battlements and embrasures. It was built in the 19th century as a private residence. In Rawnsley's time it was

Great Salkeld church, a fine example of a fortified tower

owned by a cousin of his, and one summer was let to a Mr. and Mrs. Potter whose daughter Beatrix, greatly encouraged by the young Vicar of Wray, was to win for herself a place in Lakeland's annals as prominent as that of Rawnsley himself, if not an even greater one. At least no one has yet got round to making a film of the founder of the National Trust! Eventually Wray Castle, too large to maintain in servantless times as a private house, became for a while the headquarters of the Freshwater Biological Research Association, and then, when they moved to Ferry House, Wray Castle began a new career as a training centre for mercantile marine radio officers.

*   *   *   *

The British Rail pleasure craft which carry visitors the whole length of Windermere from Lakeside reach their northern terminus when they tie up at Waterhead, Ambleside. Hereabouts, in high summer, the scene is one of intense animation, one from which the lover of Lakeland's more peaceful charms will probably wish to hasten away. Ere he does so, however, he should spare time to visit the site of the Roman camp of Galava at Borrans Field, not five minutes' walk from the pierhead. The site, 395 feet by 270 feet, was excavated by Professor Collingwood before World War I, and although, of course, only the footings of the buildings are now to to be seen, guide posts indicate quite clearly how the camp was laid out and what each of the buildings originally was. An even plainer picture emerges as a result of a visit to the Armitt Museum in Ambleside. Here there is a scale reconstruction of the fort, which was built probably during Agricola's campaign in 79 A.D., and also an absorbing collection of objects found upon the site during excavation. The siting of this particular camp, with its splendid perspective of the lake stretching away southwards between flanking hills, suggests that Windermere's beauty was not entirely lost on the reputedly dour and phlegmatic auxiliaries of Imperial Rome. It is a fitting scene to bear away as one takes one's leave of this noble expanse of water, woodland, sun and sky—crowds, promenades, ice-cream kiosks and picture-postcard emporia charitably consigned to whatever oblivion can happily be achieved. Windermere has suffered many things of many admirers but, despite all the pleasure-resort commercialisation, her age-old loveliness will keep breaking through.

STUDIES IN STONE

A FEATURE of the Lakeland scene which seldom fails to astonish and impress the visitor when he first comes to the district is that of the dry-stone walls which line the roads and lanes, separate field from field, and mark one farm's grazing rights from that of its neighbour, climbing high up the fell-sides and frequently over the top as well.

No one knows for certain when these stone walls (without mortar) first made their appearance on the Lakeland scene, but many of the longer stretches date from the Enclosure Acts of the late 18th and early 19th centuries. Some of these walls marked the boundaries of manors or townships; others kept the farmer's stock from straying (as they still do, of course) on to his neighbour's land or the public highway.

Stone-walling is a fine art of which every Lakeland farmer needs to know something, if only to keep his walls in repair. A farm with broken walling usually denotes a lazy or feckless farmer. The normal height for a stone wall used to be about 4 feet 6 inches, but modern Herdwick sheep are apparently bigger and more agile than their progenitors a century ago, and often nowadays it is necessary to stretch a strand of wire about a foot above the tops of the walls to prevent the sheep leaping over them. Especially in springtime when grazing is scarce, sheep tend to stray in search of pastures new.

Most stone walls have a rough "staircase" of long "through" stones at fairly frequent intervals. Visitors walking on the fells should use these and not weaken the walls by scrambling over them at intermediate points. Once a few stones have been displaced from a wall top, frost and rain can enter and cause a wholesale collapse.

*   *   *   *

The three north-western counties are surprisingly rich in pre-historic remains—surprisingly, that is, in view of the remoteness of the area until comparatively recent times, and in view, also, of the harshness of its climate during the winter months—longer and harder hereabouts than in most other parts of England. The cold and wet of winter can be trying enough in these days of electrically warmed and lit houses with, in many cases, double glazing, insulated ceilings and central heating. One shudders to think what living conditions must have been like, from October to May, for those skin-clad, Neolithic people of three to four thousand years ago, who built the stone circles, lived in small stone huts on open moor or fell-side, had to hunt, fish and forage for their food, and whose only source of heat and light—apart from unpredictable sunshine— were their flint-kindled fires of wood or peat.

Nevertheless, that the district was inhabited in those far-off times is testified to abundantly by the circles, cairns and hut sites which they left behind them as silent links between their generations and ours.

Probably the best-known stone circle in the Lake District is the one which stands so dramatically upon its upland site, a mile or so east of Keswick. Surrounded by the impressive bulk of both Blen-cathra and Helvellyn, although it is but a short distance from the busy main Keswick–Penrith road, the circle stands enfolded in a silence broken only by the bleating of mountain sheep and the sad, persistent calling of curlew and peewit.

This circle was once popularly supposed to have been set up in Celtic times and to have had some vague connection with Druidic rites. Locally, it was known as the Druids' Circle. Now it is known to date from a period far further back in time, though for what purpose the stones were set up it is now impossible to be certain. Did they provide a tribal meeting place, where matters of communal concern were debated and decided? Or were they connected in some way with primitive ritual observances, perhaps involving the worship and invocation of the sun? It is fascinating to speculate, but the key to any decisive answer is lacking.

Perhaps the most imposing stone circle of all in Cumbria is that which stands a few miles east of Penrith, in the parish of Great Salkeld, and is known as "Long Meg and her daughters." This is the greatest of all the northern stone circles, ranking not so far behind such megaliths of greater fame as those at Stonehenge, Avebury and the Rollrights.

Yet a third circle of great stones is that at Swinside, near Broughton-in-Furness. Because of its comparative remoteness, this fine circle is less visited than the other two already mentioned. There is no satisfactory approach road for people who must travel by car, and perhaps the grimness of the circle's surroundings, flanked as it is on almost three sides by the menacing bulk of Black Combe, accounts to some extent for its solitariness. There seems to have been an important colony in the Swinside area in Neolithic times, and the remains of several smaller circles are still to be seen within a radius of only a few miles. Further north, at Burnmoor, Seascale, Annaside, Gutterby and Kirksanton, are the pathetically small relics of once considerable circles, all of them diminished in size and number either by the action of wind or weather, or by ruthless removal, in times less pre-historically conscious than our own, in the interests of cultivation or as convenient quarries for gate-posts and stone walling.

Remains of other stone circles are sited east of the Lakes and south of Penrith, in the bleak uplands around Shap. The most famous of this group were the Shap Stones, sometimes referred to by bygone topographical writers as "Karl Lofts." Nearly every trace of this once-celebrated group has now vanished, apparently during the past two hundred years—such is modern man's genius for destruction. The fact that it once consisted of two stone circles, approached by an avenue of stones about a mile long, is only known to us because of a drawing providentially made in 1774 by the then Lady Lowther.

There are other remains of pre-historic sites in this area at Bampton, Crosby Ravensworth, Gunnerkeld and elsewhere. But how many disappeared without trace during the construction of the railway over Shap in the 1840s, and how many have been engulfed by the new M6 motorway, is a matter for sad speculation and the utmost apprehension.

*　　*　　*　　*

Among the most delightful features of the Lakeland scene, where the modern mania for motorised "progress" has suffered them to survive, are the ancient stone bridges which span many a boisterous, boulder-strewn beck.

For many centuries after the roads made by the Romans had become obliterated through disuse, neglect and over-growth, the only practicable means of transporting goods from place to place was by strings of pack-ponies. In this way the "wadd" from the Borrowdale and Honister lead mines, the woollen fleeces from many a remote dale-head farm, and sundry other saleable commodities were carried to Carlisle, Penrith, Hawkshead and Kendal markets, or to the little West Cumberland sea-ports such as Whitehaven and Ravenglass for shipment.

There were no roads between the dales—only rough "trods" or tracks, marked by stone cairns which in deep snow must frequently have been obliterated. And where, in winter, the flood-water made the becks unfordable the narrow, high-arched, rough stone bridges enabled the pack-trains to pass across in safety.

The ancient pack-horse bridges have much in common with the old stone walls of Lakeland, everywhere to be seen skirting lanes and roadways, enclosing the "intakes" round the farms, and climbing invincibly all but the highest fells. Roughly hewn from the local stone, with little or no use of mortar, the Lakeland pack-horse bridge is a thing of beauty, the product of that innate good taste which seems to have been synonymous with country craftsmanship in the days before the coming of the machine and its standardised dreariness.

Some of these bridges have been widened to accommodate double rows of motors; their parapets, originally only a foot or two high in order not to impede the bulky packs borne on the ponies' sides, have likewise perforce been raised to a higher level in the interests of safety. A few, horrible to relate, have been replaced by steel and concrete structures of a grim ultilitarian ugliness.

But many remain unspoilt, of which perhaps the most famous, and almost certainly the most photographed, is Ashness Bridge above Derwentwater on the way to Watendlath. Almost every dale can boast one or more pack-horse bridges, to enhance the scene with artefacts from a by-gone age when utility and beauty were suffered to go hand in hand.

*   *   *   *

In the grounds of a private house on the eastern shore of Windermere are some outcrop rocks which, a century and a quarter ago, were painstakingly inscribed by a craftsman of considerable skill and equally considerable eccentricity.

The engraver's name was John Longmire, and almost every day for six years, come wind come weather, he walked down the long winding road from Troutbeck to labour at his curious, self-imposed task. It is probable that the rocks then were sited in open, unenclosed land near to the water's edge. Two of these rocks are dated 1835 and 1836 respectively.

The engravings are a crazy jumble of proper names—mostly of statesmen, actors and men of letters—interspersed with impassioned pleas to Providence and sententious observations of a political character. They are clearly the outpourings of a mind deranged, though the cause of the poor fellow's mental state is unknown. Could it have been through too much ill-digested and only dimly-comprehended reading? Or had he been driven to it by the dubious dealings of the politicians of his day?

Some support for this latter theory may perhaps be deduced by the content of some of Longmire's more agonized outbursts.
"National Debt, £8,000,000. O Save my Country, Heaven!"
"The Liberty of the Press." "Magna Carta."
"1833—Money, Liberty, Wealth, Peace."—these are specimens of his lapidary exclamations.

It seems likely that the scene of Longmire's labours was a temporarily disused quarry, since some of his engravings were done on the natural rock face, others on separate slabs of riven stone lying in a variety of positions.

On a large expanse of natural rock face was carved a catalogue of famous contemporary or near-contemporary names. The list was introduced rather oddly by the word "Sun." Then followed in order the names:
"Bulwer, Dryden, Davy, Burns, Scott, Burdett, Garrick, Kemble, Gray, Kean, Milton, Henry Brougham, James Watt, Professor Wilson, Dr. Jenner"—

Longmire's tribute, apparently, to men he deemed most worthy of his praise. It is significant, perhaps, that William Wordsworth, living a few miles away at Rydal Mount, did not qualify for inclusion, though others of local distinction did so. Perhaps this notable omission can be attributed to Longmire's apparently Whiggish propensities and Wordsworth's Toryism in his twilight years.

But Whig though Longmire may have been he was clearly a patriot as well. One stone was engraved with the complacent observation, "A Slave Landing on the British Strand Is Free;" while another proudly apostrophises "George III and William Pitt, Field-Marshall Wellington, Heroic Admiral Nelson, Captain Cook, Admiral Rodney."

And was Longmire envisaging the future North Atlantic Alliance when he carved, on yet another stone, the date "1836" and the names:

"William IV, President Jackson, Louis Philippe"?

If so, he rather spoilt the effect of this gesture of international good-will by adding beneath it the uncompromising but, at that time, irrefutable statement:

"Britannia Rules the Waves."

Nor was Longmire thinking only in terms of the wooden walls which triumphed at Trafalgar for, on a stone at least eight feet square, he had inscribed in letters three feet high the one significant word STEAM."

Most of poor Longmire's inscriptions have probably now all but declined into illegibility, overgrown with grass and worn away by decades of Lake District weather. Many of the stones he carved were broken up and, it is said, used in the building of Wray Castle across the lake. But a task of such utter dedication of self may not perhaps be undeserving of posterity's notice.

* * * *

But the best-known, most often visited, most frequently photographed, single piece of stone in Lakeland must surely be the famous *Bowder Stone* in Borrowdale. It stands close to the main road a mile or so to the south of the village of Grange, and is thirty-six feet high, sixty feet long and weighs approximately twenty thousand tons.

"Bowder," of course is a Cumbrian corruption of Boulder and "some boulder" it is, as Sir Winston might have remarked. This massive, diamond-shaped lump of glacial rock has stood where it is from those far-off prehistoric times when the receding ice of the last Ice Age carried it ponderously down the glacier-hewn dale and finally left it poised improbably upon one of its pointed ends, like, as Norman Nicholson has aptly said, "a performing elephant standing on one leg."

It is said that two people lying prostrate beneath the boulder's intimidating bulk, and facing each other, can shake hands with each other, though what the purpose of this curious exercise might be is not immediately obvious. An alternative, and one would think less alarming, method of testing the Bowder Stone's immovability is to climb the wooden ladder which ascends one side of it. There used to be, and perhaps there still is, a book on the summit to be signed by those who desire thus to record their visit and their achievement.

CUMBRIAN CHURCHES

COMPARED with certain other parts of England—Somerset, the Cotswolds and East Anglia, for example—Cumbria on the whole is not a land of noble churches.* It might even be thought to be poorly endowed in this respect. Its own sadly-truncated Cathedral of Carlisle—all choir and no nave—may perhaps be considered parabolic of the area's general ecclesiological state.

There are, to be sure, the noble monastic remains of Furness, Shap and Calder Abbeys, and, still within our area or on the fringe of it, Cartmel Priory, St. Bee's Priory, Holm Cultram Abbey and Lanercost, where the parishioners who have inherited splendid fanes may be forgiven if they fluctuate from time to time between pride in their inheritance and anxiety over the costly task of upkeep.

The mediaeval monks built grandly to the glory of God, and 20th century folk still flock to visit and marvel at the material grandeur of their achievement. Less often, perhaps, do they apprehend the vision and the faith which inspired the undertaking. It is when we turn from these products of a less materialistic age than our own and consider the typical Lakeland church, that we are made aware not only of the poverty of the district but also of its remoteness until comparatively modern times.

The characteristic village church of Lakeland is of an extreme simplicity. It is usually low-walled and whitewashed, like the farm buildings of the locality; sometimes dignified with an unpretentious tower, as at Crosthwaite (Keswick), Bowness, Heversham and Grasmere, but more often without, as at Loweswater, Buttermere, Borrowdale, Cartmel Fell, Threlkeld, Wythburn, Martindale, Mungrisdale and Matterdale. The ardent ecclesiologist will look in vain hereabouts for the soaring spires of the Midlands, the lofty towers of the limestone Cotswold country, or the rich interior adornment of the great "wool churches" of Somerset and East Anglia.

*There are, of course, notable exceptions in the ancient parish churches of Kendal, Penrith, Hawkshead, Greystoke, Appleby, Kirkby Stephen and Kirkby Lonsdale.

St. Kentigern (or Mungo as he was known to his Scottish faithful) is said to have first planted the Cross, around 590 A.D., in the "thwaite," or clearing, not far from the Derwentwater island whereon, some sixty years later, St. Herbert was to have his hermit's cell. The Anglians here, as elsewhere, accepted the Faith, as did the Norsemen who came and settled among them in the 10th century. But life in the dales has been a grim struggle for existence right down the centuries and there was little wealth to spare for church building, except on the most modest scale. The "statesman's"* dwelling served as a model—four low, immensely solid walls, a green-slate roof, a deep-set porch, with the small, infrequent windows necessitated by a stern winter climate—windows offering a view which rendered unneedful the stained glass which in any case could seldom be afforded. The interior equipment would be, as it still invariably is, of the simplest kind; the only difference nowadays being that Victorian brass ornaments and pitch-pine pews predominate, though here and there the old oak benches of an earlier date have mercifully been suffered to remain.

There is often, indeed, little about a Lakeland church, apart from its size and situation, to suggest an ecclesiastical building. The successive architectural phases which are to be observed elsewhere— Saxon, Norman, Early English, Decorated, Perpendicular, Classical —are rarely in evidence in Cumbria. For long the area was so isolated and cut off from the rest of the country that fashions in building style elsewhere came and went without impact upon the dales-folk, who were content, generation after generation, to worship in the same unpretentious shrines as their fore-elders. No wealthy landowners lived in the dales; no successful wool staplers sought to express their gratitude for material blessings by raising magnificent poems in stone to the glory of God. If the great families of Cumbria who inhabited such houses as Levens, Sizergh, Muncaster, Eden Hall, Naworth or Isel (though these are not strictly in Lakeland) felt the temptation to build fine churches, they appear either to have suppressed the urge or to have confined it to their own private chapels.

The discovery of the district as a tourist attraction in the 19th century led to an increase of population, which in turn created a

---

*"Statesman," i.e. "estatesman," is the old Cumbrian name for a yeoman farmer who owned the lands he cultivated.

need for new churches in certain of the more popular resorts. To this development is due the erection of the Victorian churches of the area. These are almost invariably unimpressive and as non-memorable as the domestic and hotel architecture of the period. No Pugin, Street, Pearson or Bodley came this way to express in stone the newly-discovered principles of Gothic church architecture or the liturgical ideals of the Church Revival. Such new ecclesiastical building as there was was left to less famous and expert practitioners.* The rough grey stone of the district, appropriate enough to farm buildings, scarcely lends itself to ecclesiastical design of any pretension. The red sandstone of the outer fringes of the area, though less durable, submits perhaps a little more happily to splendour and elegance of concept.

* * * *

Cumberland, as a border county, had many centuries of anxious watchfulness, of alarums and incursions, of fleeting invasions and sharp fierce forays with marauding Scots. Something of this unsettled and often unhappy period of its history is inevitably reflected in the ecclesiastical and domestic architecture of the district, especially to the east and north of the more mountainous parts. Here was the main western highway from Scotland into England; here were the richest and most fertile Cumbrian acres where farmsteads could be attacked and pillaged, and sheep and cattle stolen and driven away northwards. During the 13th and 14th centuries, and even later, Scottish raids into Cumberland were frequent and ferocious, as no doubt were the retaliatory raids from this side of the Border which they provoked. Pele towers and fortified farmhouses and churches were for long very necessary adjuncts to North Country existence.

The fortified churches of Cumberland, indeed most Cumbrian churches which date from mediaeval times, were situated as a rule at a considerable distance from each other—an indication of the scantiness of the population in those days. Their austerity of design, lack of external ornamentation and obvious signs of repairs to the outer fabric all tell their story of churches which, like some of their bishops, found themselves engaged in warfare of a more mundane kind than that normally understood by the term Church Militant.

---

*A notable exception is Sir Giles Gilbert Scott's Gothic Revival parish church of Ambleside, but even this is not to everybody's taste nowadays.

The Abbey Church of Holm Cultram, to the west of Wigton, was one such fortified building, a fact which is emphasised not only by remains of earthworks which can still be seen in its vicinity, but also by the petition of the parishioners to Thomas Cromwell's Commissioners in 1538, when they pleaded for "the preservation and standynge of the Church of Holme Cultrane before saide; whiche is not only unto us our parish Church, and little ynoughe to receyve us all, your poore Orators, but also a great ayde, socor, and defence for us agenst our neghbours the Scots . . ."

The tower of the church of Burgh-by-Sands, near the estuary of the Solway, had walls from six to seven feet in thickness, windows with their sills eight feet from the ground, and an iron door, constructed of thick bars crossing each other and boarded over with oak planks, as the only entrance to the tower. At Newton Arlosh they made the doorway only two feet six inches wide; the windows one foot wide and three feet six inches high, with the sills seven feet from the ground.

Perhaps the finest example of a fortified church tower is that of Great Salkeld, which occupies a prominent position near the river Eden directly on an invasion route much favoured by the marauders from the North. This tower, which has been kept in a splendid state of preservation although undergoing sundry transformations down the ages, had no fewer than five floors. The ground floor was vaulted, and could be entered only from the church itself by a stout door of oak and iron. The room on the first floor has three narrow windows to provide light and also a means of observing what might be going on outside; it is also equipped with a fireplace.

Before Dearham church was "restored" in the 19th century it is said to have possessed a barrel-vaulted chamber in the lower storey of the tower, without access from the church and entered only by a small and strongly-barred doorway. When the oak beams at the top of the tower were inspected some of them showed signs of charring, and it is thought that this may have been caused through beacon fires having been lit on the tower roof by the besieged parishioners to warn the neighbourhood of another Scottish raid and of their own predicament.

In view of the constant alarms to which the inhabitants of these exposed areas were subjected in those uneasy times, it is scarcely

surprising if the older churches of the district, and particularly
their towers, are more notable for solidity of structure than for
architectural grace. The first quality to be desired was defensive
strength and other considerations were of secondary importance.
The church was most likely the only building of stone in the parish;
the only refuge to which the inhabitants could fly "when the blue
bonnets came over the Border." In those favoured villages where,
as at Brough, there was also a castle, the church was often regarded
as a kind of out-work or first line of defence. And in a few cases, as
at Barton near Ullswater, there would seem even to have been a
moat surrounding the church.

During the late 15th and 16th centuries, manor houses and even
farmhouses began to be constructed in stone; and since the ground
floor space of their pele towers often provided accommodation for
cattle in addition to that to be had above for their owners, it seems
likely that these peles to a large extent superseded the church towers
as places of refuge, particularly in the case of those who lived
nearest to them. The churches of Cumbria, nevertheless, had seen
their full share of warlike activities, and some were to continue to
do so right down to Stewart and even Hanoverian times. During the
Civil War the Cromwellians are credited, or discredited, with having
stabled three troops of horse in Cartmel Priory church, and Carlisle
Cathedral itself was similarly maltreated by the Roundheads who
pulled down the nave to provide materials for fortifying the city.
A few years later a visit from the Quaker preacher George Fox
caused a riot in the Cathedral, and troops had to be brought in to
restore order. And after the collapse of the Jacobite Rising of 1745
the Cathedral was further desecrated by being utilised as a prison
for captured Highlanders.

The residence of the Bishops of Carlisle, Rose Castle, lies seven
miles south of the city, and took shape, by stages, from the original
pele tower built by Bishop Halton in the 13th century. Like the
cathedral, Rose Castle has had its ups and downs. Destroyed by
Robert Bruce in 1322, restored by Bishop Strickland a century or
so later; captured by the Cromwellians in the Civil War and used
for incarcerating their political opponents; recaptured by the
Royalists, taken again by the Roundheads, destroyed by fire. It
was once more rebuilt by Bishops Rainbow (1664–84) and Smith
(1684–1702), but only narrowly escaped further destruction when

the Scottish Jacobites swept into England in 1745. There is a pleasant story which has it that a detachment of Highlanders, under a Captain Macdonald, was detailed to put the castle out of commission. When they arrived, however, they found a baptism in progress—that of Bishop Fleming's infant grand-daughter. Presenting the child with a white cockade, Macdonald cheerfully and chivalrously called off the attack and withdrew his men.

*   *   *   *

Cumbrian churches can show a fair selection of interesting, unusual or amusing epitaphs. In the graveyard of the ancient parish church of Bowness-on-Windermere (St. Martin's) for example, is one to Thomas Ullock, an old soldier who died in 1791, which reads:

> "Poor Tom came here to lie
> From Battle of Dettingen and Fontenoy
> in 1743 and 1745."

In Muncaster church there is a mural table to Gamel Pennington (aged eight):

> "Yes, thou art fled, and Saints a Welcome Sing,
> Thine Infant Spirit soars on Angel wing,
> Our dark affection led to hope thy stay
> The voice of God has called His Child away.
> Like Samuel early in the Temple found
> Sweet Rose of Sharon, Plant of Holy Ground,
> Aye, and as Samuel blest, to thee 'tis given
> The God he served on earth, to serve in Heav'n."

Among the memorial inscriptions in Cartmel Priory Church is an extremely terse and uncompromising one to Nicholas Barrow, who died aged eighty-three. With sharp economy of words it observes:

> "What sort of a man he was
> the last day will discover."

Barton church, near Ullswater has a touching tribute on a mural tablet to the young wife of Lancelot Dawes who died, aged twenty-two, in 1676:

> "Under this stone, reader, interr'd doth lie
> beauty and vertues true epitomy

Att her appearance the noone sun
blush'd and shrunken 'cause quite outdone
In her concentor'd did all Graces dwell
god pluck't my Rose y^t he might take a smell
Ill say noe more but weeping wish I may
Soone wth thy Deare Chast ashes come to lay."

And, as a final example, there is the often-quoted inscription in Holy Trinity parish church, Kendal:

"Here under lyeth ye body of Mr. Raulph Tirer, late vicar of Kendall, Batchler of Divinity, who dyed on 5th day of June, Ano Dni 1627.

London bredd me, Westminster* fedd me,
"Cambridge sped me, my sister wed me,†
Study taught me, living sought me,
Learning brought me, Kendall caught me,
Labour pressed me, sickness distressed me,
Death oppressed me, and grave possessed me,
God first gave me, Christ did save me,
Earth did crave me, and Heaven would have me."

* * * *

Lakeland, and more especially the southern portion of it, was the scene of no small activity on the part of George Fox, founder of the Society of Friends, commonly called Quakers. Margaret Fell, whom Fox married eleven years after the death of her first husband, Judge Fell, had come to Swarthmoor Hall, near Ulverston as a bride of seventeen—this was in 1631—and lived there until her death seventy years later.

Margaret became a Quaker in 1652 and all through the period of the Commonwealth, and then throughout the four reigns which followed it, she stood staunchly by her husband (as he subsequently became) and the teachings he so vehemently propounded. It is not surprising that with Swarthmoor Hall as the Vatican, so to speak, of Quakerism, Quakers and Quaker Meeting Houses proliferated in the Furness and Cartmel areas.

---

*i.e., Westminster School.
†This has been taken to mean that his sister persuaded him to marry, and possibly produced a suitable bride.

Keswick and Derwentwater from Latrigg

Perhaps the most famous of the Meeting Houses is that built in 1688 by George Fox himself. It stands beside Swarthmoor Hall and contains many interesting relics of the eloquent preacher and the Judge's widow he had married.

The earliest of the Quaker meeting houses were of the greatest simplicity—plain rectangular buildings, white-washed without and austerely furnished within. Open rafters roofed with rough slate slabs from the fellsides were all that intervened between the heads of the faithful and the skies above. This sparse severity was meant to provide the utmost contrast with the idolatrous "steeple houses" of the Anglican Church, with their altars, fonts, pulpits, lecterns, stained glass and mural tablets. This contrast they invariably succeeded in achieving, but for all their barrenness there was in most cases a quiet dignity about their whitewashed walls, slate-flagged floors, rough oaken benches and square-paned windows of plain glass.

In the present century Quakerism has experienced a considerable decline in numbers. From many of the dales where once its adherents were numerous the last Quaker family has disappeared. Only in some of the larger centres of population are there congregations of any size. Kendal, once a stronghold of the Friends, still has its Meeting House and there are others at Grayrigg, Colthouse, Arnside, Yealand and Preston Patrick.

The Furness area from Hawkshead southwards was once full of Quakers. One of the earliest meeting houses was that at Colthouse, half-a-mile from Hawkshead. The first interment in its burial ground took place in 1652.* This was many years before Fox initiated the building of the Meeting House at Swarthmoor.

In the burial ground of the old Meeting House at Tirril, between Penrith and Pooley Bridge, lie Thomas Wilkinson, friend of the Wordsworths and owner of the spade which the poet once apostrophised in verse; John Slee, who in his time was a mathematician of note; and Charles Gough, whose tragic death on Helvellyn was commemorated in verse by both Wordsworth and Sir Walter Scott.

Not far from Cartmel Fell, high up above the lovely Winster

---

*This attractive little building still has its original oak panelling and wooden gallery. When I visited it recently electricians were at work installing modern strip lighting. *O tempora!*

Ulverston: Market Place

Valley, was the Meeting House known as the Height Chapel, built in 1667 but long since abandoned. Standing over a thousand feet above sea-level, it was one of the outcomes of the Five Mile Act of Charles II's reign which made it illegal for any non-conforming worship or teaching to take place within five miles of any town. The The Meeting House at Rook How, in the Rusland Valley, was founded in 1725.

* * * *

Two of three miles north of Cockermouth, and on the northern bank of the river Derwent, stands the church of St. Bridget, long since "Cumbrianised" into Bridekirk. St. Bridget was one of those early Irish saints of whom the Vikings learned in their voyagings, and in whose honour they dedicated churches in the Lake Counties.

The old, pre-Norman church of St. Bridget stands in ruins, amid other ancient stones which witness to a centuries-old Christian occupation of this hallowed site. But for all its comparative modernity, the present church houses the most satisfying piece of antiquity of them all. This is an ancient, pre-Norman font, with its fascinating carved representations of dragons and other fabulous monsters. Of more religious significance are portrayals of the Baptism of Christ, and of the expulsion of Adam and Eve from the Garden of Eden. On the side the sculptor has executed a self-portrait, accompanied by carvings of a mallet and chisel and a runic inscription by way of signature.

In *A Description of England and Wales*, a work published in 1749, it is stated that the font was found among the ruins at Papcastle and that the inscription on it had long proved a puzzle to antiquaries. One of the most learned of these, however, William Nicolson, Bishop of Carlisle from 1702 to 1718, believed that it should be read as *Er Ekhard han men egrocten, and to dis men red wer Taner men brogten;* which he translated as:

"Here Ekhard was converted; and to this man's
example were the Danes brought."

A later historian of the Lake Counties, W. G. Collingwood, preferred a somewhat different reading. He rendered the inscription as:

Rickarth he me wrokte, and to this merthe gernr me brokte,—
"Richard he me wrought, and to this beauty eagerly me brought."

Rickarth, according to Collingwood, was Master Richard of Durham, a 12th century craftsman of great reputation in northern England. This would seem to pose further problems rather than clarify matters, but the curious visitor can take his choice.

It is perhaps worth mentioning, as a footnote, that at Bridekirk Vicarage were born Sir John Williamson of the family who owned Millbeck Hall, near Keswick, and Thomas Tickell, poet and friend of a greater poet, also of Cumbrian descent, Joseph Addison.

THE LAST EARL OF DERWENTWATER

VISITORS to Keswick's lovely lakeside are often intrigued to learn that one of the largest of the islands, tree-covered and separated from the shore by only a narrow stretch of water near Stable Hills Farm, is known as Lord's Island. Inquiry leads to the information that it is so called because upon it once stood the home of the Radcliffe family, three members of which bore the title of Earl of Derwentwater. The visitor will also almost certainly be told that, early in the 19th century, stones from the ruined mansion were used in the re-building of Keswick's picturesque Moot Hall.

A local legend of highly doubtful historicity has long delighted to tell how, when her husband, the third Earl, lay condemned to death in the Tower of London, the Countess of Derwentwater crossed one dark night from the island to Stable Hills Farm bearing with her the Radcliffe family jewels. The story then tells how the Countess proceeded to scale the not very lofty but extremely precipitous slopes of nearby Walla Crag, and from there made her way to London, by way of Kendal, to plead for her unfortunate husband's pardon and release.

A romantic and picturesque tale but not, alas, a very likely one. The route said to have been taken by the Countess, still known locally as "The Lady's Rake,"* would provide a stiffish climb for a modern mountaineer, wearing the appropriate gear for the exercise, in broad daylight. For a delicately nurtured noblewoman, at dead of night and clad in 18th century costume, it does not appear to have been a feasible kind of achievement. In any case, the mansion on Lord's Island is known to have been ruinous and uninhabited long before 1715, the date of the Countess's legendary exploit.

Reluctant though one may be to demolish so appealing a story, historical truth ought not to be tampered with, and the true facts concerning the last of the Derwentwaters are surely sufficiently dramatic as to render recourse to fiction otiose and unwarranted.

*"Rake," a word frequently met with in Cumbria, is Norse for a steep mountain path or track.

They relate to happenings of high political significance on a national scale, leading to a tragic *dénouement* of truly classical proportions.

And now—to turn from the legendary and the romantic to harsh historical fact.

Many visitors to Keswick inspect with interest the 16th century Radcliffe family tomb in Crosthwaite Church with its brass effigies and inscription. This tomb marks the burial place of Sir John Radcliffe, and commemorates also his wife Dame Alice, who survived him and is actually buried in Salisbury Cathedral. The two 15th century alabaster effigies which lie beneath the stone slab bearing the brasses are not of Sir John and his wife. They are of two unknown persons of the period, and originally were sited elsewhere in the church. When the Victorian "restorers" got to work in the 15th century, they did some "tailoring" on the effigies, in order to force them between the pillars supporting the slab of the Radcliffe brasses—doubtless in order to provide room for yet more pews.

This Sir John Radcliffe, incidentally, is supposed to have led a contingent of Keswick men to fight at the battle of Flodden in 1513. The Radcliffe family had for some centuries owned Lord's Island, and are believed to have been Lords of the Manor of Keswick as far back as the reign of Edward I. A Radcliffe fought and died with Richard III at the battle of Bosworth Field in 1485. The Radcliffes had founded the family fortunes on the ownership of the Newlands Mines, for the working of which German miners were brought to Keswick from Augsburg in the reign of Queen Elizabeth I.

There were Radcliffes also in Northumberland, and to make clear all the ramifications of this highly prolific family would call for the skill of an expert genealogist. We need not concern ourselves now with this aspect of the family's antecedents, except to say that their principal seat was at Dilston Castle, three miles to the south-east of Hexham. This they had acquired through marriage in the 15th century. Further marriages united them with other notable Northumbrian families such as the Fenwicks, Lawsons and Greys, and with the brides, of course, came lands and wealth.

The Radcliffes had always been Roman Catholics and Royalists —"recusants" in the eyes of the law at that time—and Francis Radcliffe was created a Baronet by King James I in spite of having been suspected of complicity in the Gunpowder Plot. The second baronet, Sir Edward Radcliffe, further enlarged the family possessions by judicious purchases and by an even more judicious marriage to a rich heiress, Elizabeth Barton, of Whenby in Yorkshire. Less judiciously, perhaps, but with creditable loyalty, he fought for his King in the Civil War and suffered the sequestration of his estates under the triumphant Cromwellians. They were, however, restored to him when "the King came into his own again." He died in 1663, and was succeeded as third baronet by his grandson, another Sir Francis.

This Sir Francis was now one of the most considerable land-owners in the North of England, and he set his sights very high indeed in looking for a wife for his eldest son Edward—no less than one of King Charles II's natural daughters. There was, admittedly, a fair range of choice of these, and in 1672, when Edward was only sixteen, his father was negotiating for the hand of Lady Charlotte Fitzroy, daughter of the King and Barbara Villiers, Duchess of Cleveland. Nothing, however, came of this idea, possibly because the prospective bride was only eight years old—though such considerations were not usually regarded as of much account when a a *mariage de convenance* was being discussed. At any rate, it was not until twelve years later that Sir Francis's great ambition was realised when a marriage was solemnised between Edward Radcliffe, now thirty-one, and Lady Mary Tudor, aged fourteen, daughter of the King and the actress Mary, or Moll, Davis.

This was in 1687 and the bride's father had been dead for two years. Her uncle, James II, was now on the throne and as co-religionists the stock of the Radcliffes stood high with the King, quite apart from the marriage connection. A few months later, James raised Sir Francis Radcliffe to the peerage with the titles of Baron Tyndale in the county of Northumberland, Viscount Radcliffe and Langley, and Earl of Derwentwater in the county of Cumberland.

A few months later still came the Revolution of 1688, which dethroned King James and put his daughter Mary and his son-in-law, William of Orange, on the throne in his place.

As a known Roman Catholic recusant, the new Earl of Derwentwater was regarded with some mistrust by the Government of King William in London, and soon they were receiving reports from their agents in the North of highly suspicious gatherings of armed horsemen at Dilston Castle. Nothing of a seditious nature seems to have been proved, however, and for a time the Earl was left in peace. Then, in 1691, he was committed to prison for a period by order of the magistrates at Northumberland Quarter Sessions.

The first Earl of Derwentwater died in April, 1696, and was succeeded as second Earl by his son Edward, he who had married Lady Mary Tudor. This second Earl only survived his father nine years. He died in April, 1705, at the age of 49, leaving three sons: James, aged sixteen (born in 1689), Francis, aged fourteen (born in 1691); and Charles, aged twelve (born in 1693). It is with James, third Earl of Derwentwater, that we are mainly concerned of these three sons. There was also a daughter, Mary, who was born in 1697 and in 1721 married William Petrie of Bellhouse, in the county of Essex.

The children's mother, Lady Mary Tudor, had separated from her husband, the second Earl, in 1700 because of differences over religion, and when he died in 1705 she remarried—her second husband being Colonel Grahme of Levens, who had been a close friend of King James II, Keeper of the King's Privy Purse, Deputy Lieutenant of the Castle and Forest of Windsor, and Member of Parliament for Carlisle. It was this Colonel Grahme who employed King James's French gardener, M. Beaumont, to design and lay out the famous gardens and topiary work at Levens.

But to return to the Radcliffes—the third Earl, aged sixteen, and his fatherless brothers and sister. Having lost their mother as well, by her separation from their father and then by her second marriage, they were virtually orphans. In 1702, James, the eldest boy, and his youngest brother Charles (they were then thirteen and nine respectively) had been sent for protection to St. Germain-en-Laye, to the Court of the exiled James II and his Queen, Mary of Modena. The young Prince of Wales (later to be known as "the Old Pretender") was the same age as his cousin, the third Earl of Derwentwater, and the two lads seem to have been constant companions, sharing the same tastes and of course the same religious faith and upbringing. It is even possible that they shared the same tutors. Or it may be that the young Earl was sent for the completion of his education to the Jesuit College of St. Louis-le-Grand in Paris, where his kinsman William, afterwards fourth Lord Widdrington, was being educated. In between studies there would no doubt be sundry gaieties to divert the young men, though, in fact, both the Prince of Wales and his cousin the Earl of Derwentwater showed signs of piety and seriousness of outlook unusual for lads of their age.

King James II had died in exile in September 1701, and his supplanter and son-in-law, William of Orange, a few months later, on March 9th, 1702. This meant that James's younger daughter Anne was crowned *de facto* Queen of England, while across the water at St. Germain-en-Laye, the Jacobites in exile proclaimed her half-brother James as *de jure* King. Queen Anne was Anglican in her religious allegiance; her half-brother had been brought up a strict Roman Catholic. Anne, who was married to the amiable but colourless Prince George of Denmark, had borne him seventeen children, but not one of them survived beyond infancy.

It was known that Anne would have liked her young half-brother to succeed her on the throne, but unfortunately his religion was against this. By the Act of Settlement of 1701 it was enacted that, in default of legitimate issue to Queen Anne, the Crown of England was to go to the nearest Protestant heir, the Electress Sophia of Hanover, grand-daugher of James I, while another clause in the Act required that the Sovereign must, in future, be in communion with the Church of England. And so, failing a Repeal of the Act of Settlement by the English Parliament, which appeared improbable, James's prospects of becoming King seemed remote. Had he consented to change his religious allegiance, like his great-grandfather, Henry of Navarre, who thought "Paris was worth a Mass," it would no doubt have been a different story. But James, to his credit, firmly declined to do this.

For his Jacobite supporters there remained but one alternative— to stage an invasion and, hoping that a sufficient number of English, Irish and Scottish Jacobites would rise in support, to seize the capital and proclaim James in place of his half-sister Anne. It was a desperate alternative, but many of the Jacobites were desperate men who had little to lose by failure and everything to gain by success. They knew that there was a considerable amount of pro-Jacobite feeling in Ireland, Scotland, Wales, and in the North and West of England. They also expected solid support, in the shape of money, men and arms, from King Louis XIV of France, who had his own reasons for wishing to see a Roman Catholic Stewart back once more on the throne of England.

THE LAST EARL OF DERWENTWATER   173

There was a great deal of intrigue and plotting at St. Germain and incessant coming and going of Jacobite spies and agents from across the water. The young Earl of Derwentwater would be fully aware of all this and before long, as a kinsman and co-religionist of the Pretender to the throne, he inevitably found himself involved in what was going on.

In 1705, when he was sixteen, he left St. Germain in order to complete his education by making the Grand Tour of Europe. It seems to have been a leisurely affair, even for those unhurried times, and when he returned from it, early in 1708, he found plans already far advanced for an attempt at invasion. The Act of Union between England and Scotland had been passed in the previous year, and had aroused a good deal of bitter feeling on both sides of the Border. Sir Winston Churchill, in his great life of his ancestor, the first Duke of Marlborough, wrote, "Highland clansmen, Whig noblemen, Covenanters, Catholics and Presbyterians, were all ripe for rebellion, though with different objects. Now, if ever, was the hour for the rightful heir to Scotland's ancient crown to set foot upon Scottish soil."

So, also, thought the Jacobite exiles at St. Germain. So, also, did King Louis, whose armies were being hard-pressed by Marlborough. A French fleet of twenty-five ships was assembled at Dunkirk, together with twelve battalions of troops and a large quantity of arms to equip the Scottish Jacobites. Charles Fleming, a brother of the Earl of Wigtown, was sent on ahead to proclaim James when he arrived and to arrange a code of signals for use between the French ships and their sympathisers on shore. On the 28th February, Louis went to St. Germain to present James, who was to accompany the expedition, with a diamond-hilted sword. He said to him: "The best wish I can wish you is that I may never see your face again!"

On March 9th James arrived at Dunkirk and promptly caught measles. He recovered, however, and on March 17th he was carried, wrapped in blankets, on board the flagship *Mars*. It was on this somewhat unpropitious note that the invasion fleet set sail. The winds were favourable and the ships were rapidly driven towards the south-east coast of England. The following day they were sighted off Lowestoft by an English fleet under Admiral Byng, but Fourbin, the French Admiral, gave this fleet the slip and sailed on past the Firth of Forth until, just off Montrose, he sighted Scotland. Then they beat back into the Firth of Forth where James pleaded to be set ashore. By this time, however, Byng had caught up with them, and Fourbin realised that if he was not to be hopelessly trapped he must leave the Firth. The French ships put out to sea and after a running fight, during which one ship, the *Salisbury*, was captured by the English, they eventually succeeded in getting back to Dunkirk.

Aboard the captured *Salisbury* were many notable Scottish Jacobites, among them the young Earl of Derwentwater and his brother Charles. Many of the leaders captured on board were kept in prison until 1712, but the Earl and his brother, together with several other less prominent Jacobites, were sent back to France on parole. It was an ignominious end to the invasion attempt, and much of the blame for the failure must undoubtedly rest with the French Admiral who had been so unwilling to risk the loss of his ships. Had he succeeded in landing the troops and arms on Scottish soil, the attempt to restore the House of Stewart in that year of 1708 might very well have succeeded because there were almost no Government troops in the country to resist them. The major part of the British Army was on the Continent, winning victories under Marlborough. As so often before and afterwards, the Jacobites had come within inches of success only to have it dashed from them because of someone's treachery, muddle or failure of nerve.

In the summer of 1709, the Earl of Derwentwater was twenty years of age and he applied for, and somewhat surprisingly was granted, a licence to return to England. He is described as being "of middle height, with fair hair and grey eyes, and a noble and pleasing countenance." He had received a good education in France and could talk intelligently upon a wide variety of subjects. He was also a good musician with a pleasant singing voice and, like some young men of the present day, when singing he liked to accompany himself on the guitar. But one imagines that the songs he sang were of a somewhat different kind! He seems to have settled down quite happily at Dilston Castle, to which he proposed to add some extra buildings. He entered fully upon the life of a country gentleman of the time, hunting and shooting, and paying courtesy calls on local families. Among these were the Widdringtons, of Widdrington Castle, near Morpeth, a building now vanished, its former site being occupied by a farmhouse. The Radcliffes were related to the Widdringtons, and

William, later the fourth Lord Widdrington, as we noted, was at school in Paris when Derwentwater was living at St. Germain.

In spring of the following year, 1710, the Earl visited his estates in Cumberland, and it is interesting to picture him riding across with his retinue from Dilston to Keswick, via Penrith. One wonders whether he came by Alston or by Stainmoor. It may well have been by Alston, where he had a considerable financial interest in the Lead Mines, in which hundreds of men were employed. It would be natural that he should wish to inspect them from time to time. Contemporary sources pay tribute to the Earl as a man who stood high in the affections of his neighbours, tenants and dependants, as a good landlord, a liberal host in his own house, and generous in his benefactions to the deserving and needy. Although so firmly attached to his own religious beliefs, he was no bigot and made no distinction between Catholic and non-Catholic when distributing his benefactions.

On the 10th July, 1712, he married Anna Maria, daughter of Sir John Webb, Baronet, of Canford in Dorset and Heythrop in Gloucestershire. He had known his bride since she was a child, for she had likewise been educated in Paris, at the Augustinian Convent there, and had been received at the Court of St. Germain. For the next two years the young couple lived at Heythrop, in one of the houses owned by the bride's father. This was while the alterations and additions were being made to Dilston Castle. These were partially completed by the early part of 1714, enabling the Earl and his Countess to take up residence. But the new western wing, which was to contain the principal reception rooms, was still unfinished and in fact was destined never to be completed. According to the Victoria County History, the ancient tower was incorporated into the new structure, and this tower alone still stands. The hall was paved with marble of black and white chequered design. To the west and south of the house were formal gardens, while the stables were on the north side of the mansion. From this rear side of the house, a carriage drive led out under a clock-tower, down the hill to Devilswater, which it crossed by a bridge built in the 17th century and known as "the Lord's Bridge." On the south side was a spacious park, full of deer. Through this park ran another drive, at the end of which were gates flanked by stone pillars. The chapel inside the house was dedicated to the Blessed Virgin, and contained many of the family tombs.

Frank Radcliffe, the elder of the Earl's two brothers, died unmarried in May, 1715, while Charles, the younger brother, was living, it would appear, a somewhat dissolute life in London, a fact which caused the Earl considerable distress. A son and heir, John, had been born to the Earl and Countess just before they had taken up residence at Dilston.

*   *   *   *

Ever since the abortive attempt in 1708 to place the son of James II on the English throne, Jacobite plotting and preparations, in Britain and in France, had gone on incessantly. Led by Bolingbroke and the Duke of Ormonde in France, by Sir William Wyndham and Lord Lansdowne in England, and by the Earl Marischal in Scotland, the Movement had been steadily gaining ground, especially in the West and North, as Queen Anne's health deteriorated and the prospect of a German princeling as King loomed nearer. If only the calibre of their leaders had been of a higher quality, the Jacobites might well have succeeded in having the Pretender proclaimed as James III when the Queen died on Sunday, 1st August, 1714. As it was, the Whigs were more efficiently organised, more determined, and quicker off the mark. While the Jacobites still havered and hesitated, and while James in Paris wasted precious hours discussing what colour sealing-wax he should use on his royal correspondence, the Whigs had their man over from Hanover and proclaimed as George I.

In spite of this serious set-back, however, the Jacobites continued to plot and intrigue on behalf of the Pretender and to drink their enigmatic toasts to the "King over the Water," or to "£3 14s. 5d." (James III, Louis XIV and Philip V of Spain).

Derwentwater, though temperamentally a man of peace, happy in his family life, in his home, his estates and country pursuits, was naturally sympathetic to his cousin's cause and ready to do what lay in his power to advance it. He seems to have been a member of a Jacobite secret society which called itself the "Corporation of Walton-le-Dale" and which met under a cloak of conviviality to pursue its political purpose—the restoration of a Stewart to the British throne. The so-called "Corporation" consisted of many of the Catholic and Jacobite gentry who were well represented in the Northern Counties of England. It used to meet at the Unicorn Inn at Walton which, ironically enough, had served as Cromwell's northern headquarters in 1648. In 1709, the "Mayor" of the pseudo-Corporation was the then Duke of Norfolk, and in 1711 it was James, Earl of Derwentwater.

There was an abundance of Jacobite fervour in many parts of England, as well as in Wales, in Ireland and the Highlands of Scotland. The accession of German George was greeted with pro-Jacobite riots in Oxford, Wolverhampton, Leeds, Manchester, Warrington and elsewhere. In Somerset many church bells were rung on the Pretender's birthday, 10th June, and he was openly toasted in many places. At Gloucester, a Mr. Samuel Hayward, who protested publicly at the anti-Hanoverian behaviour of the crowds in the streets, was set upon, badly beaten and barely escaped with his life.

The principal drawback to James's cause, apart from his religious persuasion, was the lack of a really competent leader around whom his supporters in this country could rally. Had they had anyone of the quality of Montrose or Claverhouse, or with the glamour of the "Young Pretender", to inspire and organise them and to direct their enthusiasm to practical purposes, the outcome of the Rising of 1715 would undoubtedly have been different.

Superficially, all the circumstances favoured the Jacobites. George I had been on the throne only a short time. He spoke no English, cared little for England, and he and his hordes of German hangers-on were almost universally disliked. The standing army was no more than 16,000 strong, and of this number only about half were available in this country. And, as a consequence of the rioting in the provinces, the Government had revived the Riot Act of 1553, a move which did nothing to promote the popularity of the regime.

Abroad, as we have seen, Louis XIV more or less openly supported the Jacobite claims, and although by the Treaty of Utrecht he had undertaken not to allow James a refuge on French soil, he obligingly turned a blind eye to the Pretender's residence in the dependent territory of Lorraine, barely a hundred miles from Paris. The Queen Mother, Mary of Modena, was still allowed to maintain her court at St. Germain, on the outskirts of Paris, and this of course was an ever-active centre of intrigue. Jacobite letters to friends and supporters in England were carried by French diplomatic couriers among their official papers, and Louis even encouraged his grandson, Philip V of Spain, to contribute 400,000 crowns to the Jacobite cause. James's half-brother, the Duke of Berwick, who was one of the most able soldiers of the day, was always available to offer valuable advice.

Unfortunately for his cause, James was usually more inclined to listen to the advice of less competent mentors, such as the Duke of Ormonde and the Earl of Mar. Apart from Berwick, who had lived all his life abroad and knew nothing of conditions in England, the only realistic adviser James had was Queen Anne's former Minister, Bolingbroke, who favoured a rising in England rather than in Scotland. One of Bolingbroke's difficulties, even after his flight to France, was in making contact with James. Only a hundred miles separated them, but the spies of the English Ambassador, the Earl of Stair, watched every movement of Bolingbroke in Paris. When he wrote to the Prince, these spies seized his couriers on the road to Lorraine and abstracted his letters. Even when cyphers were used they were so transparent that they deceived no one. By this means the Government in London was kept informed of almost every move the Jacobites proposed to make long before they were in a position to make it.

The death of Louis XIV on 1st September, 1715, was a crushing blow to James. He had been the Pretender's best friend in Europe. The new Regent, the Duke of Orleans, was much more anxious to keep on good terms with the British Government. Meanwhile, acting on Stair's information the two English Secretaries of State, Stanhope and Townshend, had despatched a naval squadron under Admiral Byng to watch the French ports. Twenty-one new regiments of infantry were raised, and strong garrisons were installed in those West of England towns, such as Bristol, Oxford, Bath and Plymouth, where Jacobite sympathisers were known to be most numerous. The *Habeas Corpus* Act was suspended for six months and a number of prominent Jacobites, among them several Members of Parliament, were arrested on charges of attempting to promote a Rising in the West.

In Scotland, where the Earl of Argyll had been given command of the Government forces, the Earl of Mar was the spear-head of all James's hopes. The Pretender could have been better served. The sixth Earl of Mar, "Bobbing John" to his contemporaries, was personally brave, but erratic, lethargic and militarily incompetent. He was persuaded by the weak state of the Government's forces in Scotland into a premature raising of the Jacobite standard at Braemar on 6th September. Thereafter he proved himself utterly incapable of organising the revolt he had precipitated, or of exploiting an initially favourable situation to his master's advantage.

The northern Jacobite plan was that when Mar raised the flag of revolt in the Highlands, there was to be a rising in the Lowlands under the leadership of Lords Kenmure, Nithsdale, Carnwath and Wintoun. They were then to be joined by sympathisers in Cumberland and Northumberland under Thomas Forster, M.P. and the Earl of Derwentwater. These were then all to march northwards and join up with Mar's forces for an attack upon Argyll. At the same time the Duke of Ormonde was to land from France in the West of England at the head of a force of exiled Jacobites.

With a greater share of luck and under more resolute and competent leadership, the plan could have resulted in a spectacular success. What actually happened was that Ormonde's movements were betrayed to the Government, so that when he reached the Devon coast he found no Jacobite supporters waiting to greet him and strong Hanoverian forces not far away. Understandably in the circumstances, he re-embarked and returned whence he came.

Meanwhile, the Earl of Mar, with about ten thousand Highlanders, had advanced towards Dunblane to settle accounts with Argyll, whose total strength was a little over 3,000 men. On 13th November they met at Sheriffmuir, a mile and a half north-east of Dunblane and a few miles north of the key-town of Stirling. The result of the battle which followed was unsatisfactory and indecisive. The right wing of each army drove in and defeated the troops opposite to it. Even so, had Mar possessed even a modicum of military ability he could successfully have exploited the situation. Instead, hearing that Dutch and Swiss mercenaries had been landed at Leith to reinforce Argyll, he weakly fell back on Perth, all advantage lost or abandoned. He failed utterly to appreciate that in a rebellion a retreat is usually as fatal as a defeat.

We must now return to events in the Lowlands of Scotland, and over the Border in Northumberland. Towards the end of September the Earl of Derwentwater had received news that a warrant for his arrest had been issued by the Secretaries of State in London, and he decided that it would be wise for him to leave Dilston for the time being. He stayed first with a friend, Sir Marmaduke Constable and then, to avoid compromising Sir Marmaduke, he went to live in disguise at one of the cottages on his extensive estate. When the news of the raising of the Jacobite standard at Braemar reached him and his fellow Jacobites in the neighbourhood, they deemed that the time had come to appear in arms in the Pretender's cause. A rendezvous was arranged near Corbridge and here, on 6th October, the Jacobites assembed under the command of Thomas Forster. This man was an even less competent military leader than the Earl of Mar, and did not even share the Earl's quality of courage. He had only been chosen as leader of the Northumbrian Jacobites because of his position as a Member of Parliament, and because he was the only eminent Jacobite in the county who was not a Roman Catholic.

There were some sixty horsemen in the party, mostly local gentlemen and their servants, and as they moved in the direction of Newcastle which they hoped to capture their strength was gradually increased by new arrivals. At Warkworth they proclaimed King James III, and then advanced on Morpeth where more recruits joined them. They failed in their plan of taking Newcastle for lack of infantry, and because the Whig magistrates of that city had hurriedly repaired the breaches in the crumbling outer walls. It never seems to have occured to Forster to dismount his men and attack the city on foot.

Instead, they turned westwards towards Hexham, and then northwards, where they joined up first with Lord Kenmure's contingent and then, at Kelso, with the main Lowland force under General MacIntosh. This was on 22nd October. According to plan they should now have headed north to make a junction with the Earl of Mar. Had they done so, Argyll would have been so heavily outnumbered that all Scotland must inevitably have fallen into their hands. Instead, they moved westwards to Langholm, with the intention of launching an attack on Dumfries which was known to be in a defenceless state.

Divided councils now caused confusion and uncertainty in the

Jacobite ranks. The Scots were for seizing Dumfries, Ayr and Glasgow, where little opposition was to be expected. They could then have struck across country towards Stirling and taken Argyll and his small force in the rear. Lord Derwentwater would seem to have favoured this plan or, as an alternative, doubling back on Newcastle where it was now known that General Carpenter had only 900 men to defend the city. "General" Forster, however, thought otherwise, and since it was he who held James's commission as leader, his view prevailed. They would march south into loyal Lancashire, where it was believed at least twenty thousand Catholic Jacobites were ready to join them. With such a force, Forster reckoned, they could then confidently march on London.

And so this brave little band of less than a thousand Scots and English country gentlemen, with little or no military experience, allowed themselves to be persuaded. It was to prove a fatal mistake.

On 1st November, All Saints' Day, they were at Brampton; the next day, they moved towards Penrith, where they proclaimed King James III and seized or tried to seize the Salt Tax Money but otherwise comported themselves with exemplary decorum. From Penrith they advanced, by way of Appleby, Kendal and Lancaster, to Preston.

The Jacobite cavalry entered Preston on 9th November, and the infantry the following day. Here they were joined by about 1,600 sympathisers, ill-armed and undisciplined. They were probably a poor enough replacement for the 500 or so Scots who had deserted at Appleby and had retired quietly back across the Border. The insurgents contemplated continuing on their way to Manchester, where it was known that Jacobite supporters were numerous and active. A rapid and decisive march would most likely have meant the town falling into their hands, but once again precious time was frittered away. Their opponents were given a chance to close in, and the opportunity passed.

As soon as the threat to Newcastle had been lifted by the Jacobites' southward march, General Carpenter had emerged from the town's defence works and proceeded to shadow the invading force. Another force under General Willis had moved up rapidly from the south and had secured Manchester. Then, with several regiments of cavalry and some battalions of infantry, he invested Preston from the south as Carpenter's troops approached the town from the north.

Had the Jacobites been under competent leadership they could no doubt still have given the attackers a considerable amount of trouble and anxiety. But Forster lacked the rudiments of such ability, and failed to take even the most elementary precautions. No attempt was made to defend the bridge over the Ribble, and all the defenders were concentrated in the centre of the town behind street barricades and loop-holed houses.

Willis attacked on 12th November with horse and foot, while the Lancashire Militia under Colonel Houghton made a diversion near the East Cliff. The spear-head of Willis's attacking force was the 26th Foot, later the First Battalion of the Cameronians, and they found themselves up against MacIntosh's Highlanders. A ferocious action took place, largely in the churchyard of Preston parish church where, wielding claymore and Lochaber axe, the clansmen repulsed the Hanoverian troops with heavy losses.

The next day Carpenter arrived and was astonished to find the bridge across the river undefended. A few score determined men could have held this bridge against an army, but as soon as Forster had heard of the approach of Carpenter's contingent he had withdrawn all his men into the centre of the town. Now the Jacobites were pressed in on every side, and only two options remained open to them—to try to cut their way out of the encircling ring, or to surrender. The Earl of Derwentwater, who had fought valiantly all the previous day stripped to the waist, was in favour of the first alternative, and so was his brother Charles. Forster, however, had no taste for such heroics and, without consulting any of his colleagues, sent messengers to Willis proposing a capitulation. When this was known in the Jacobite ranks there was an outburst of rage and a deep sense of having been betrayed. For a time, Forster's life was in danger from some of his own followers. The Jacobites, however, were ordered to lay down their arms, Lord Derwentwater and Colonel MacIntosh were handed over as hostages, and the remainder of the insurgents were disarmed by the Government troops.

And so, on the very day that the fiasco of Sheriffmuir was being fought in Scotland, this even greater fiasco was taking place at Preston. Nearly 1,500 Jacobites were captured, of whom more than 1,000 were Scots. In the brief action of the previous day, however, they had given a good account of themselves for whereas only 17 of James's men were killed, about 200 Hanoverian soldiers fell. A large number of these were men of the Lancashire Militia, who would seem to have received the main brunt of the Highlanders' onslaught.

The prisoners, Lord Derwentwater among them, were kept under strong guard in various local inns and churches. Then those of rank were taken under escort to London, while the remainder were tried in various northern towns such as Lancaster, Kendal and Carlisle. Some were executed, and hundreds of others transported for life to the American plantations. The armed party escorting the high-ranking Jacobite prisoners was met at Highgate by a detachment of Guards. The captives were made to ride two abreast, a soldier with fixed bayonet leading each horse; the escorting cavalry all with drawn swords, the infantry with drums beating. Lord Derwentwater and some of the other leaders were lodged in the Tower of London; Forster, Charles Radcliffe, MacIntosh and others in Newgate Goal.

When he was captured at Preston, Lord Derwentwater told his huntsman to take his favourite grey horse and, if possible, make his way to Dilston, there to secure and destroy the family papers and any other documents which might incriminate others. The huntsman found an unguarded side street by which he was able to slip away from Preston, and then, by way of the hills to the east of the town and the Lune Valley, the gallant horse bore him all the way to Dilston. Arriving there on a dark November afternoon, he broke the news to Lady Derwentwater of her husband's capture and of the Jacobite defeat. The family papers were hastily packed and sent away that night to the neighbouring mansion of Capheaton, the home of the Catholic Sir William Swinburne, where they were concealed in one of the house's seven "priest holes," the one in question having been constructed between two walls, behind a chimney.

The Countess of Derwentwater at once set out for London—a 300 mile ride on horseback, over the roughest of roads, in the deep mid-winter. Lady Nithsdale, whose husband had also been taken at Preston, set out about the same time on the same kind of journey, and she wrote afterwards, "The season was so severe, and the roads so extremely bad, that the post itself was stopped. But we managed to get horses and rode to London through the snow, which was generally above the horse's girth." It is to this period, of course, that the legend of the Countess of Derwentwater's flight from Lord's Island by way of "the Lady's Rake" is supposed to refer. But in fact the Countess was at Dilston when the disastrous news from Preston reached her, and the house on Lord's Island, as already mentioned, had been in a ruinous condition ever since the Civil War in the middle of the previous century.

Lady Derwentwater was allowed to share the Earl's imprisonment in the Tower until the 9th of January, when she obtained permission to move out because in the next apartment the Lady Catherine Wyndham was lying ill with small-pox. Various attempts were made by the Countess and others to obtain a royal pardon for the Earl, but they all foundered upon King George's insistence that the prisoner should renounce his Roman Catholic Faith and acknowledge the House of Hanover as rightful wearers of the British crown. On neither of these conditions was Lord Derwentwater prepared to purchase his life. At his trial before Parliament in Westminster Hall on 9th February, 1716, he had pleaded Guilty to being in arms against King George and to having assisted in a warlike act of invasion, but protested that he had at no time intended any harm against his Majesty King George's person. He also reminded the Court that he had been given to understand that if he surrendered peaceably to the King's officers at Preston his life would be spared.

All this, however, availed him nothing. Sentence was passed that he, together with Lords Widdrington, Nithsdale, Carnwath, Kenmure and Nairn, be hanged, drawn and quartered according to the barbaric usage of the time. In the cases of Derwentwater, Kenmure and Nithsdale, this savage sentence was commuted to one of beheading, and the executions were fixed for the 24th February, on Tower Hill.

Further unavailing efforts were made to save the condemned men, and Sir Robert Walpole boasted that he had been offered £60,000 if he could obtain the King's pardon for the Earl of Derwentwater. A Petition in favour of the prisoners was even introduced into the House of Commons and Walpole, who had been most active in crushing the rebellion, only secured its rejection by a majority of seven. The warrant for the execution of the three men (Carnwath, Widdrington and Nairn having already been granted a respite) was signed by the Elector on 23rd February. That night

Lord Nithsdale escaped from the Tower disguised as his wife's female servant. Lords Derwentwater and Kenmure were not so fortunate, and the next day mounted the scaffold where they paid the ultimate penalty for their loyalty to the House of Stewart. Both died with great dignity and courage, commending their souls to God and expressing forgiveness to all men.

The Earl's last wish had been that his body might be taken to Dilston for burial, but this request had been refused by the authorities for fear of stirring up popular feelings against the Hanoverians in the North. Nevertheless, his friends did contrive to obtain possession of it and to smuggle it northwards, travelling by night and resting by day. The Earl's embalmed body was in this way brought back to his own country and amid the sorrowful lamentations of his kinsfolk, friends and tenants laid to rest in the little chapel of the castle where he had so often worshipped.

All the Derwentwater estates in Cumberland and Northumberland were taken into sequestration by the Crown and awarded to Greenwich Hospital, and when the Commissioners of the Hospital, in 1874, decided to dispose of the Dilston portion of them, the third Earl's remains were removed from the chapel and re-interred at Thorndon in Essex, in the family vault of Lord Petre, a descendant through marriage. Most of the castle would seem to have been demolished about the year 1775.

For several nights after the Earl's execution and burial there were remarkably vivid displays of the *Aurora Borealis*, and by the simple Northumbrian peasantry these displays were accorded a supernatural significance. For many years thereafter this phenomenon was known locally as "Lord Derwentwater's Lights."

*   *   *   *

It might perhaps be argued that, by the prevailing standards of the time, the English Government behaved towards the defeated and captured insurgents with comparative clemency. In addition to the Earls of Derwentwater and Kenmure, twenty-four other leaders of the Rising were executed. There might well have been more, but for the fact that Lords Wintoun and Nithsdale escaped from the Tower, and Forster, Charles Radcliffe, Brigadier MacIntosh and Robert Hepburn of Keith from Newgate.

Of the rank and file, some seven hundred were brought to trial and sentenced to transportation. In 1717, by an Act of Indemnity, Lords Carnwath, Widdrington and Nairn, who were still in the Tower, were set at liberty, together with a number of other Jacobites under sentence of death.

The causes of the failure of "the Fifteen" are obvious enough—divided counsels, inadequate resources, incompetent leadership, lack of sufficient foreign support and loss of nerve on the part of the English Jacobites. The consequences of the failure were a steady consolidation of the Hanoverian dynasty under Walpole's firm guiding hand, and a progressive increase in the nation's prosperity. This in turn made further political adventures on behalf of the Stewarts a prospect with an ever-diminishing appeal to practical-minded Englishmen. The failure of "the Fifteen" not only settled the first two German Georges securely upon the throne of Britain, but it virtually deprived the House of Stewart of its last practicable opportunity of recovering its fallen fortunes.

* * * *

Some verses said to have been written by the Earl of Derwent-water on the eve of his execution may perhaps be considered a not unsuitable epitaph upon this gallant but ill-fated young nobleman.

> Farewell to pleasant Dilston Hall,
>   My father's ancient seat:
> A stranger now must call thee his,
>   Which gars my heart to greet.
> Farewell each friendly well-known face,
>   My heart has held so dear:
> My tenants now must leave my lands
>   Or hold their lives in fear.
>
> No more along the banks of Tyne
>   I'll rove in autumn gray:
> No more I'll hear at early dawn
>   The lav'rocks wake the day.
> Then fare thee well, brave Witherington
>   And Foster ever true,
> Dear Shaftesbury and Errington
>   Receive my last adieu.

And fare thee well, George Collingwood,
  Since fate has put us down:
If thou and I have lost our lives,
  Our King has lost his crown.
Farewell, farewell, my lady dear;
  Ill, ill, thou counsell'dst me:
I never more may see the babe
  That smiles upon thy knee.

And fare thee well, my bonny gray steed,
  That carried me aye so free,
I wish I had been asleep in my bed
  The last time I mounted thee.
The warning bell now bids me cease,
  My trouble's nearly o'er;
Yon sun that rises from the sea
  Shall rise on me no more.

Albeit that here in London town
  It is my fate to die,
O carry me to Northumberland
  In my father's grave to lie.
There chant my solemn requiem
  In Hexham's holy towers,
And let six maids of fair Tynedale
  Scatter my grave with flowers.

And when the head that wears the crown
  Shall be laid low like mine,
Some honest hearts may then lament
  For Radcliffe's fallen line.
Farewell to pleasant Dilston Hall,
  My father's ancient seat;
A stranger now must call thee his,
  Which gars my heart to greet.

The Earl's only son is believed to have died in 1731, at the age of nineteen. His only daughter married, at the age of seventeen, Robert James, eighth Lord Petre. Charles Radcliffe, the Earl's younger brother, was arrested for his part in the Rising of 1715, but contrived to escape to France. A few years later he returned to this country and married the widowed Countess of Newburgh, by whom he had three sons and four daughters. Although then over fifty years of age, Charles was prepared to take an active part in the Jacobite Rising of 1745. He sailed for Scotland in November of that year in a French frigate bound for Montrose with stores, ammunition and volunteers for Prince Charles Edward's army. Unluckily, a Hanoverian frigate, the *Sheerness*, was met with off the Dogger Bank and the French ship was forced to surrender. With the other Jacobite officers on board, Charles Radcliffe was taken to London and imprisoned in the Tower. Not until a year later was he put on trial for high treason in Westminster Hall. In spite of his claim to be a subject of the King of France, in whose army he had for some years held a commission, Charles was found guilty and was executed on 8th December, 1746.

There have been over the years various claimants to the Derwentwater title and estates, but none has ever been substantiated. The estates, in any case, came under attainder after the third Earl's execution and, as already mentioned, were conficated and bestowed upon Greenwich Hospital. In 1787, as an act of partial restitution, a rent charge upon the estates of £2,500 per annum was granted to Anthony James, Earl of Newburgh, Charles Radcliffe's grandson. The Earl died without issue in 1814, the last heir male of the Derwentwater family.

Other descendants of Charles Radcliffe, by his three sons and four daughters, there undoubtedly were, and there was even one lady who claimed title and estates on the grounds that she was descended from John, son of the ill-fated third Earl. She was the Countess of Waldsteine and her claim was that, so far from having died in 1731 as was commonly believed, John Radcliffe had escaped to Germany where he had married the Countess of Waldsteine and died at the age of 86. The lady, who claimed to be his grand-daughter, came to England in 1868 and actually "squatted" for a time in the ruins of Dilston Castle, with a retinue of servants in attendance. Eventually she was persuaded to withdraw by Mr. Grey, the Receiver to the Greenwich Hospital Estates, and the lady's claims were subsequently heard of no more.

finis

INDEX